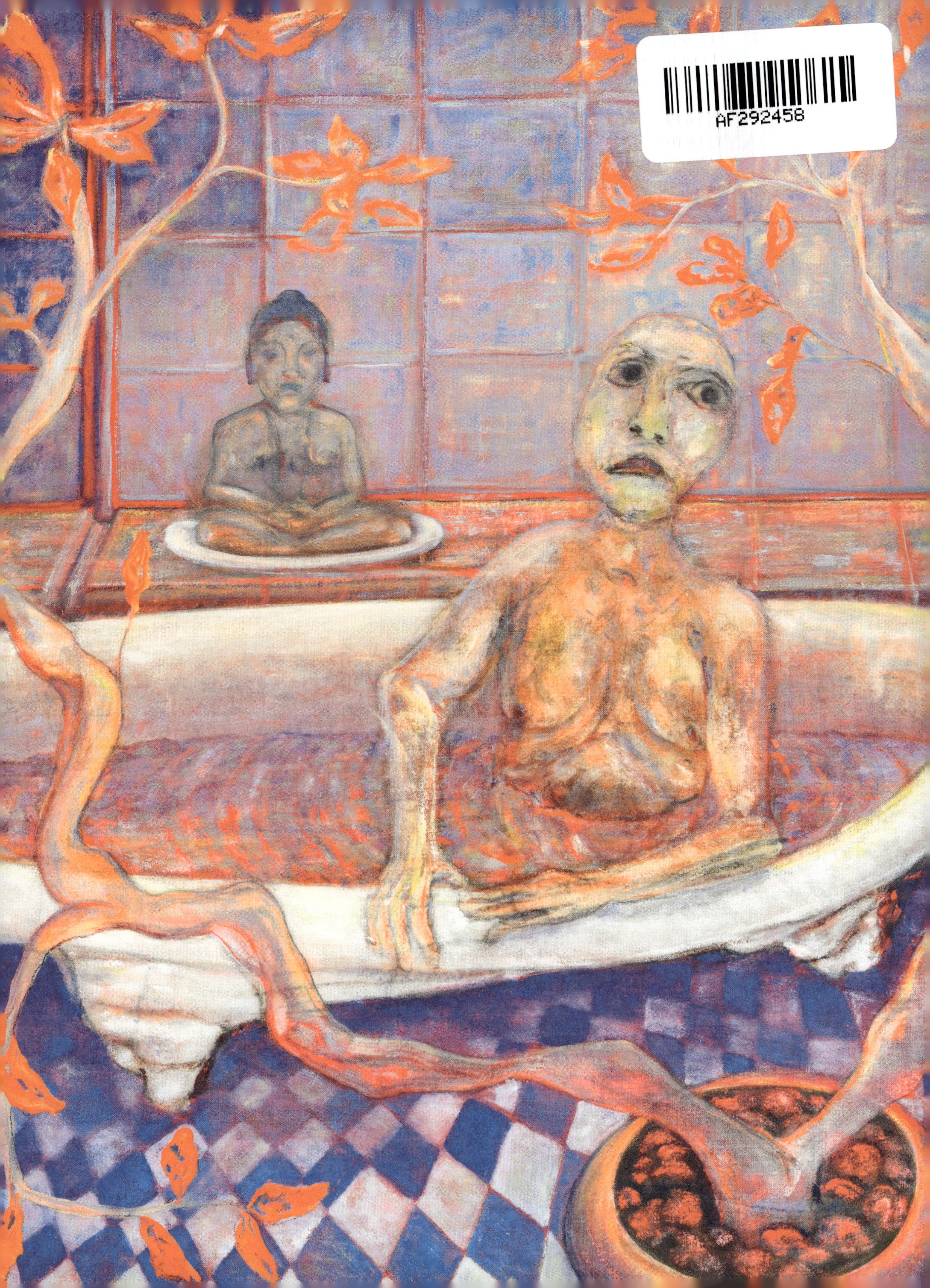

AF292458

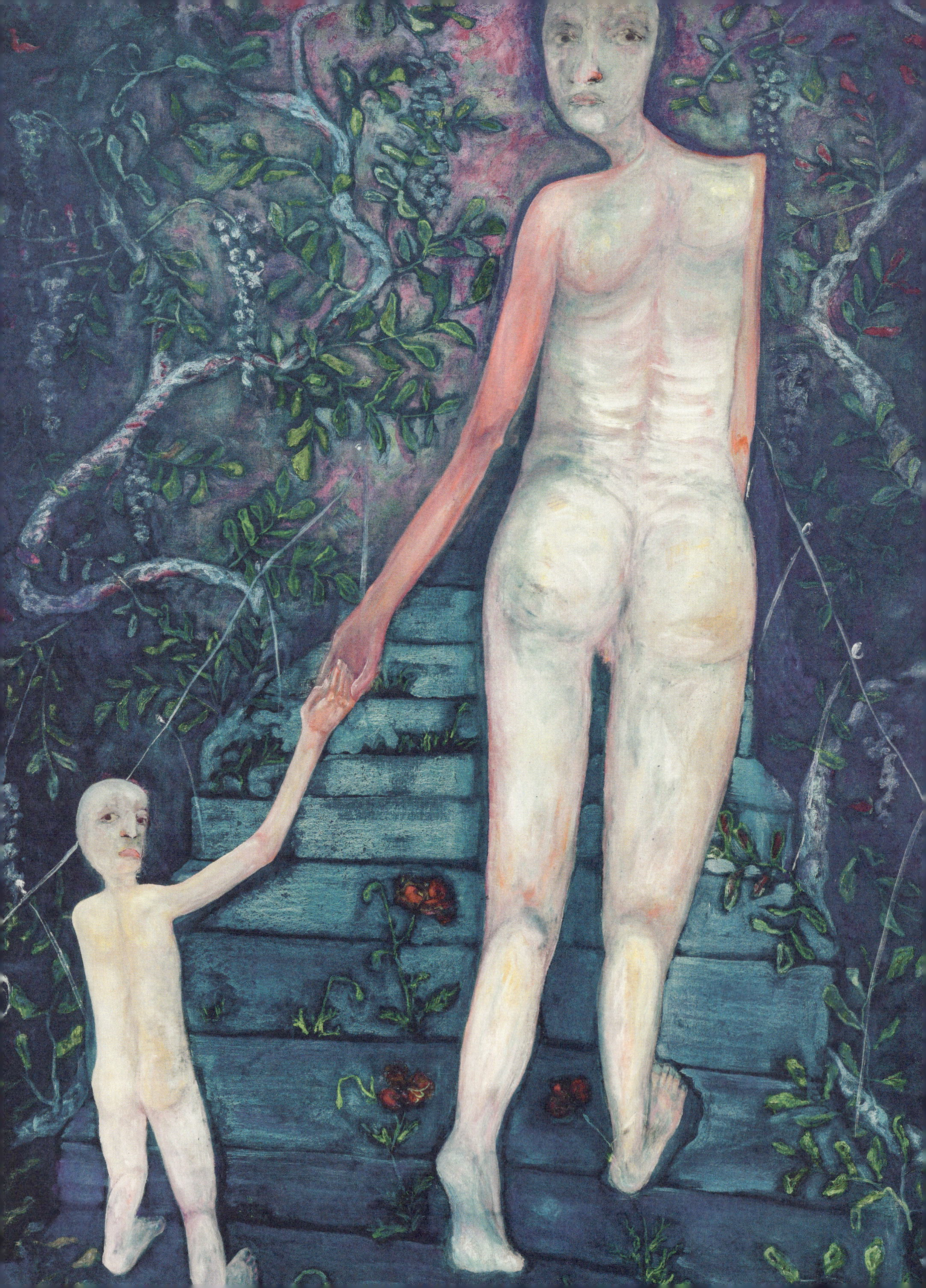

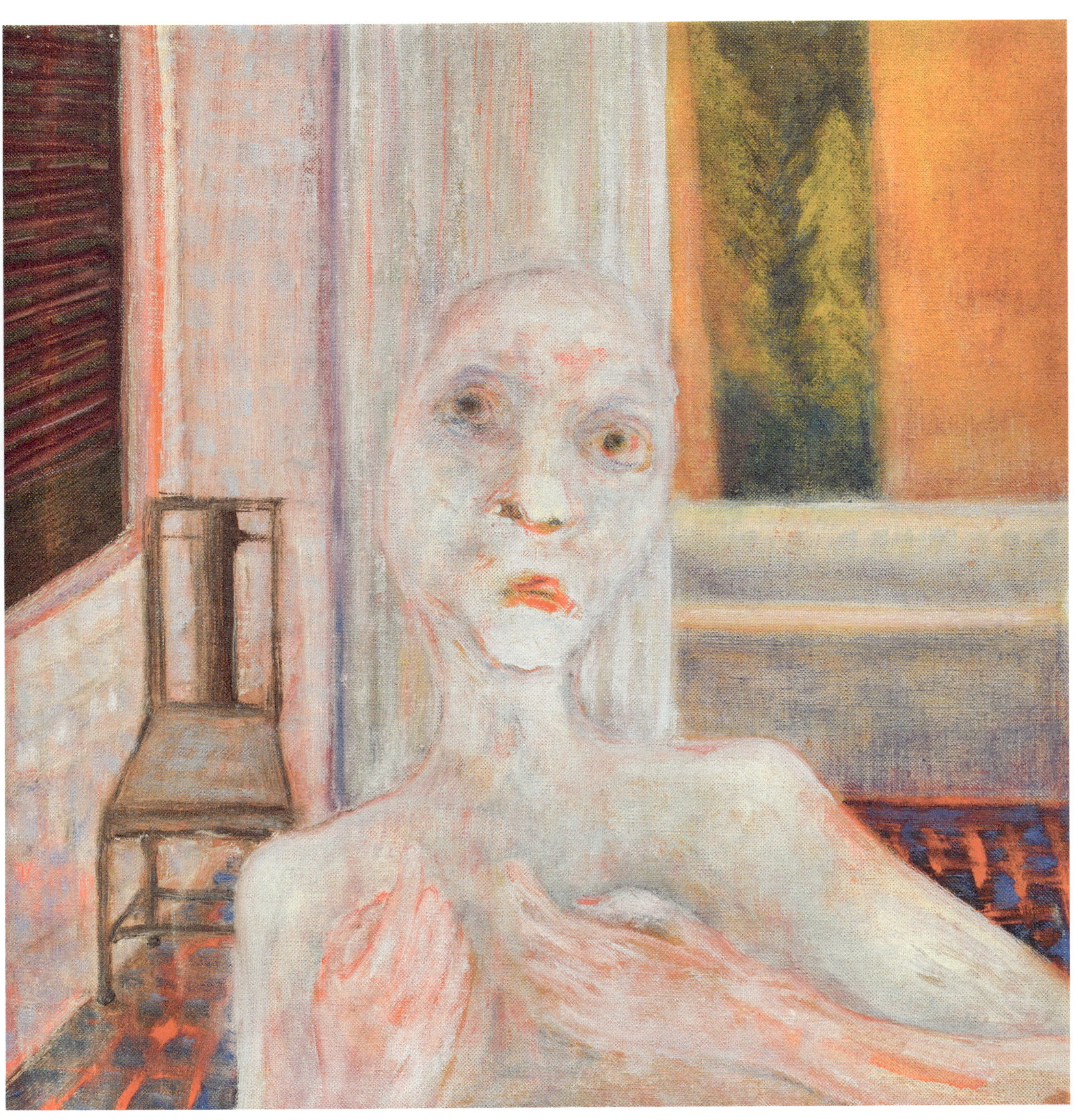

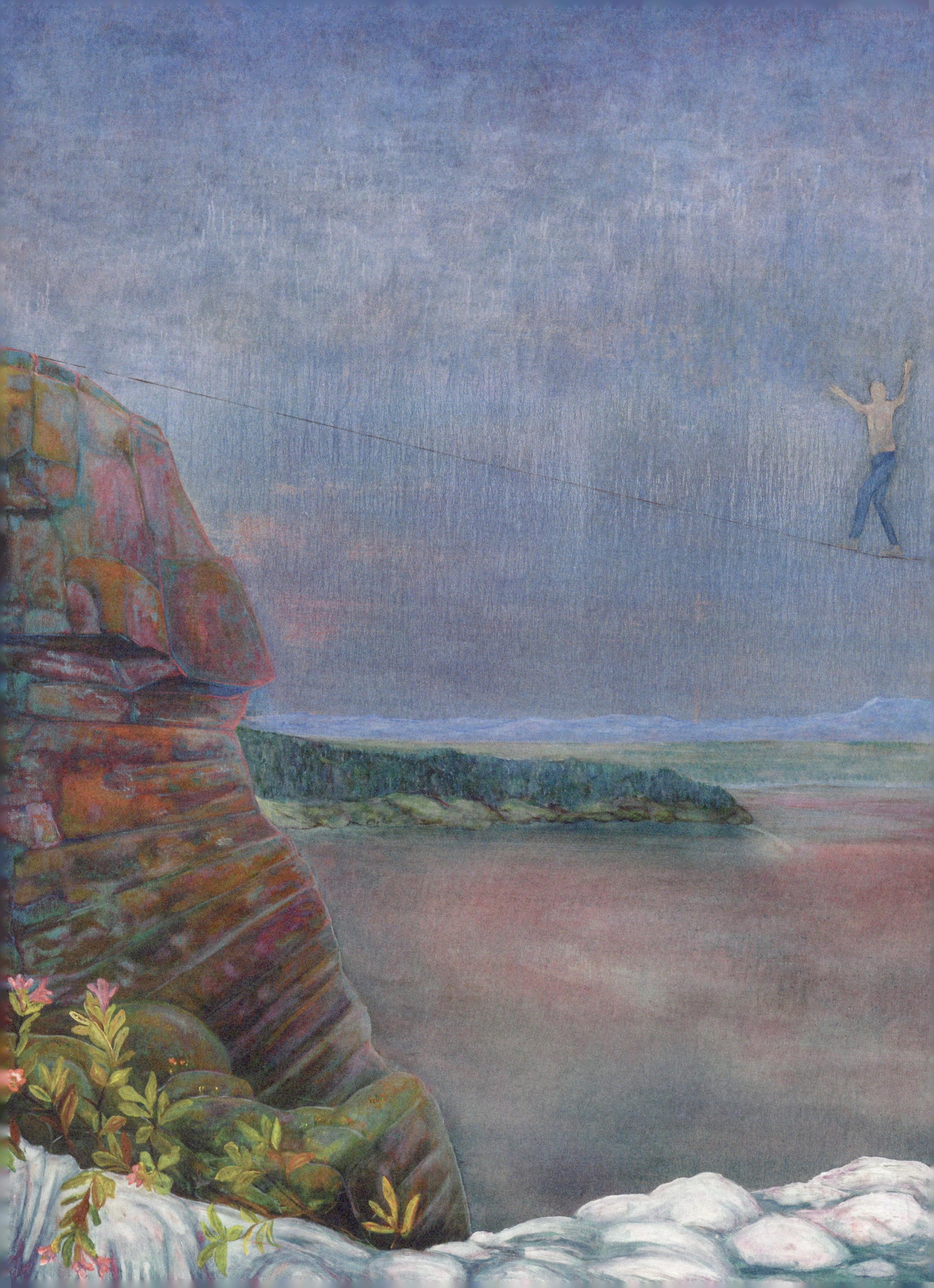

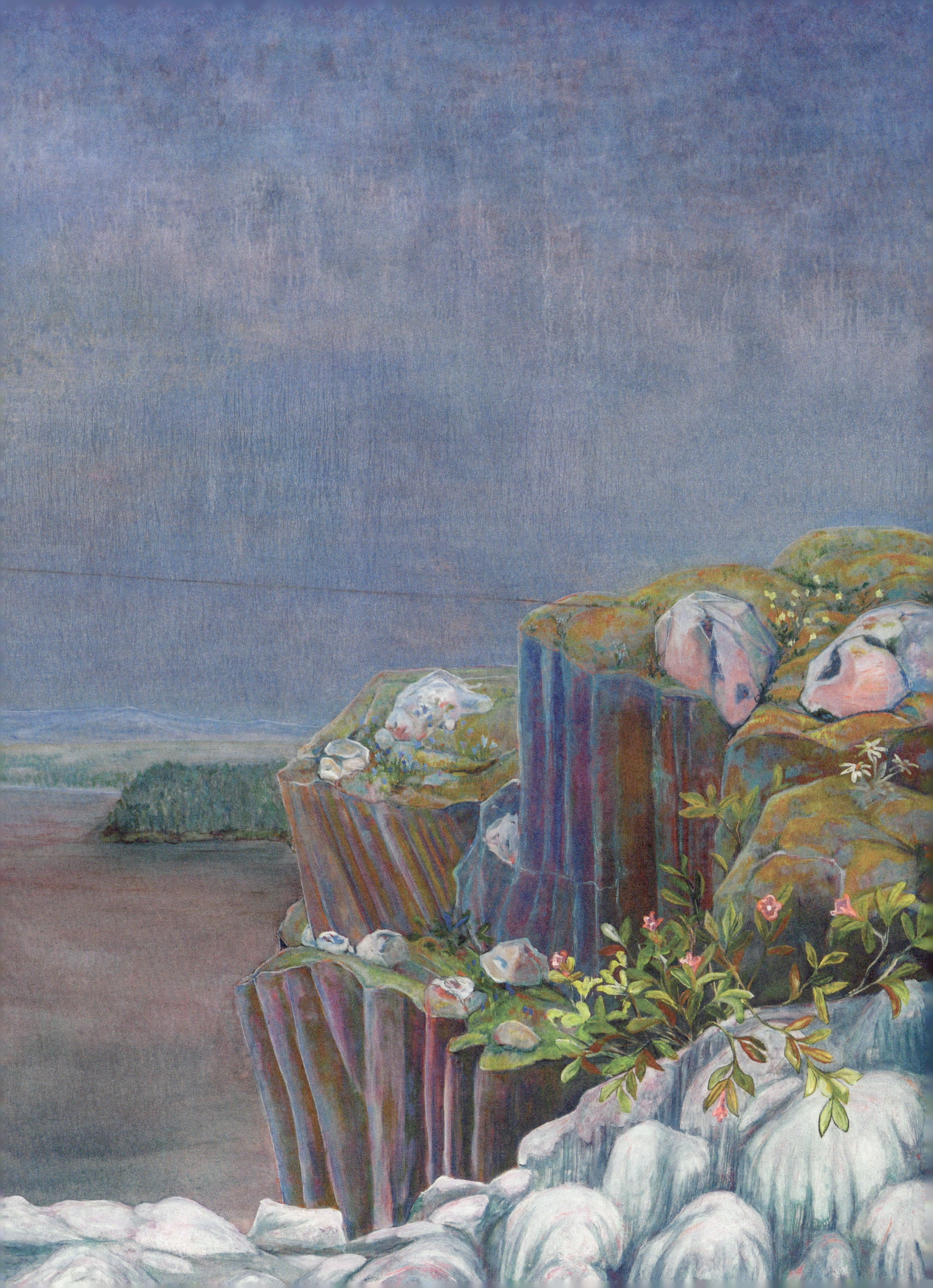

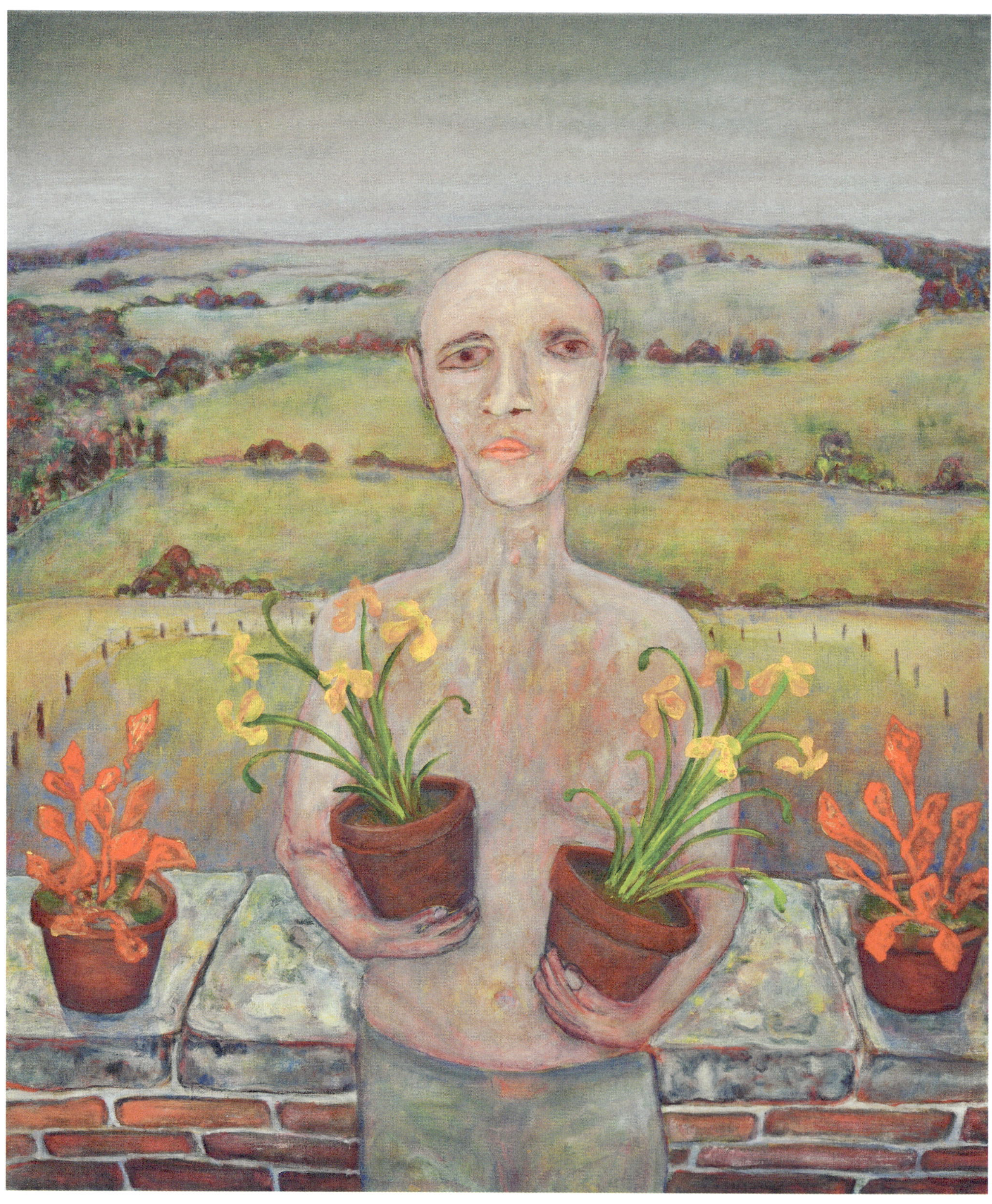

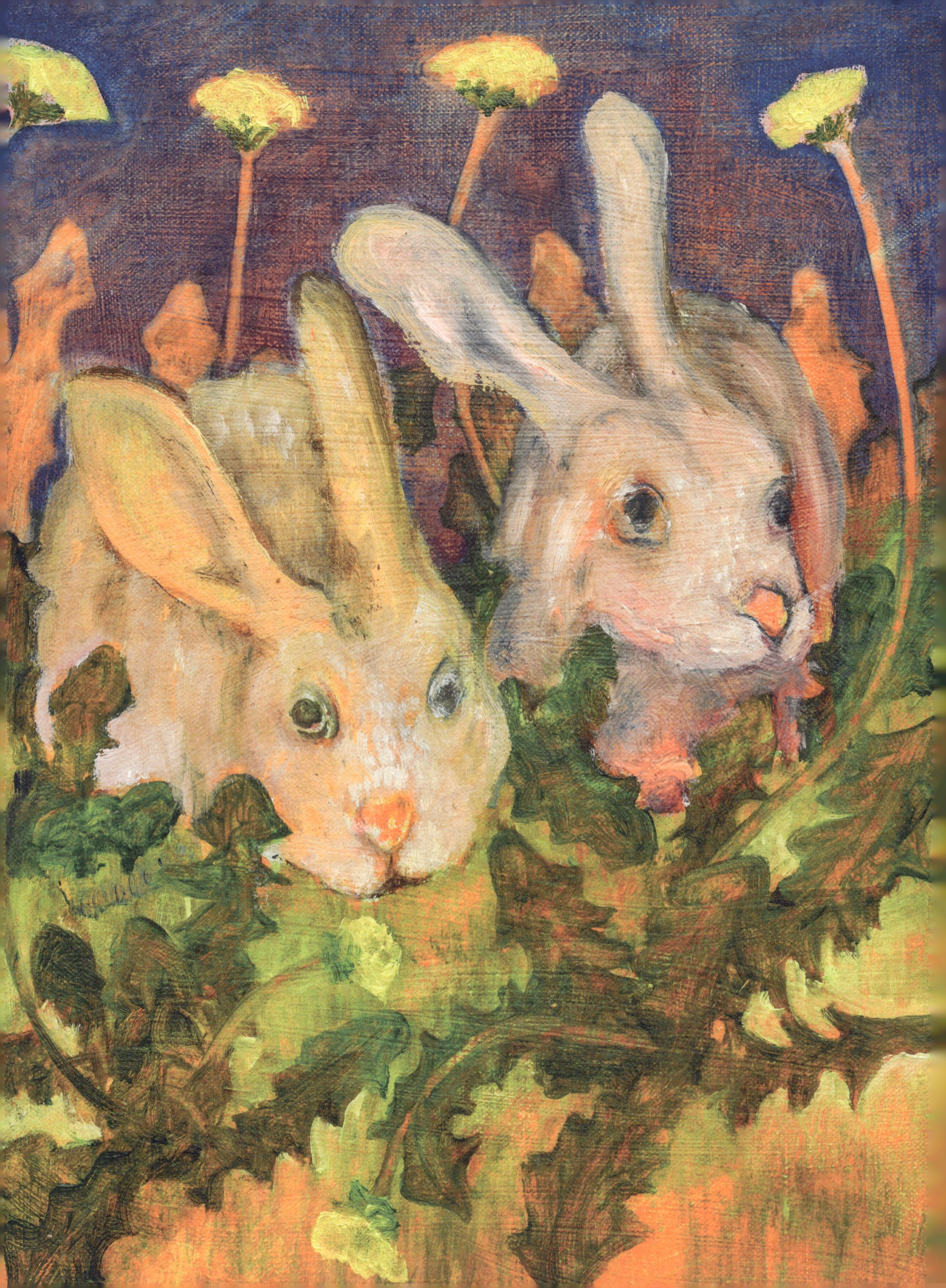

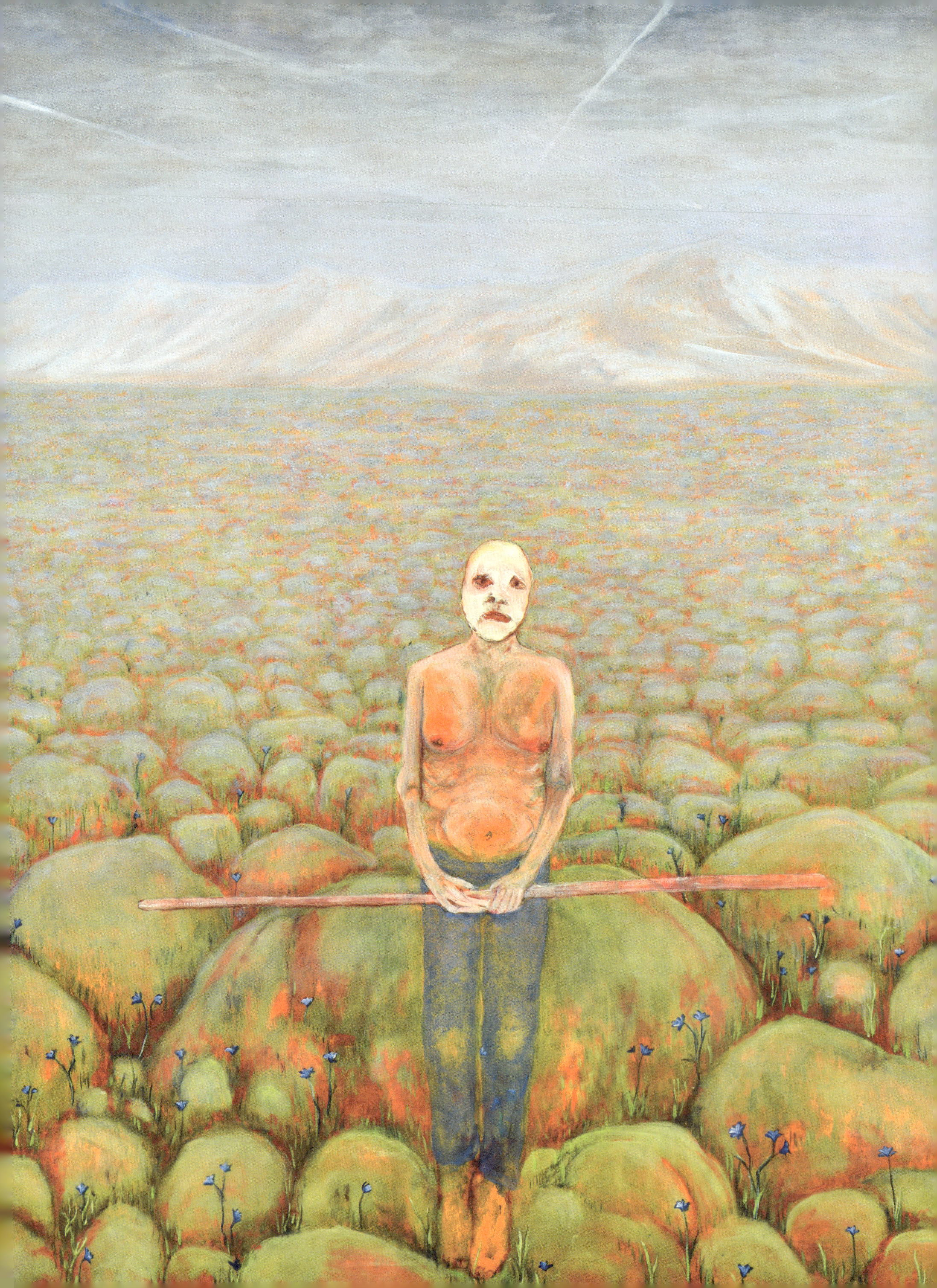

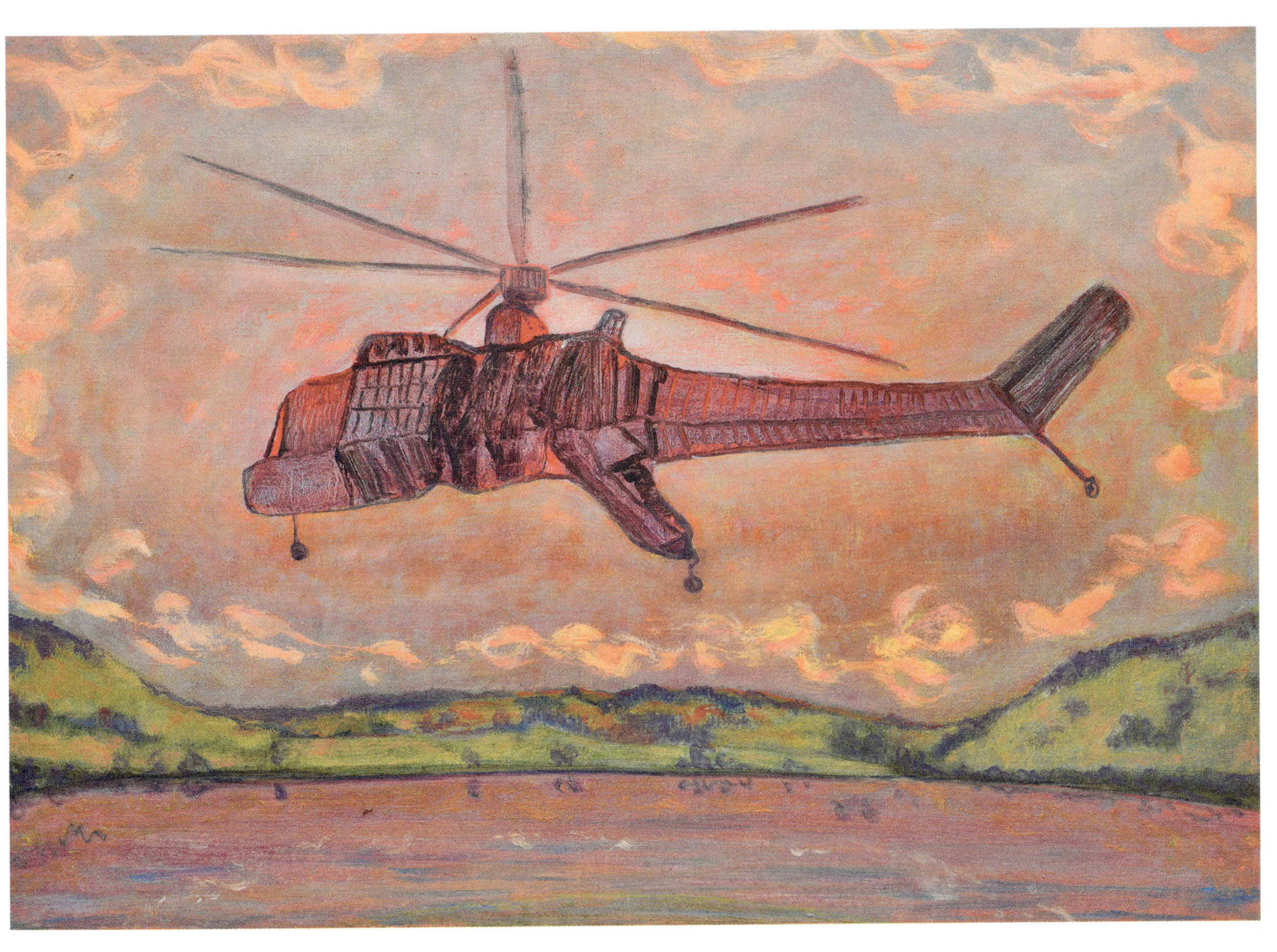

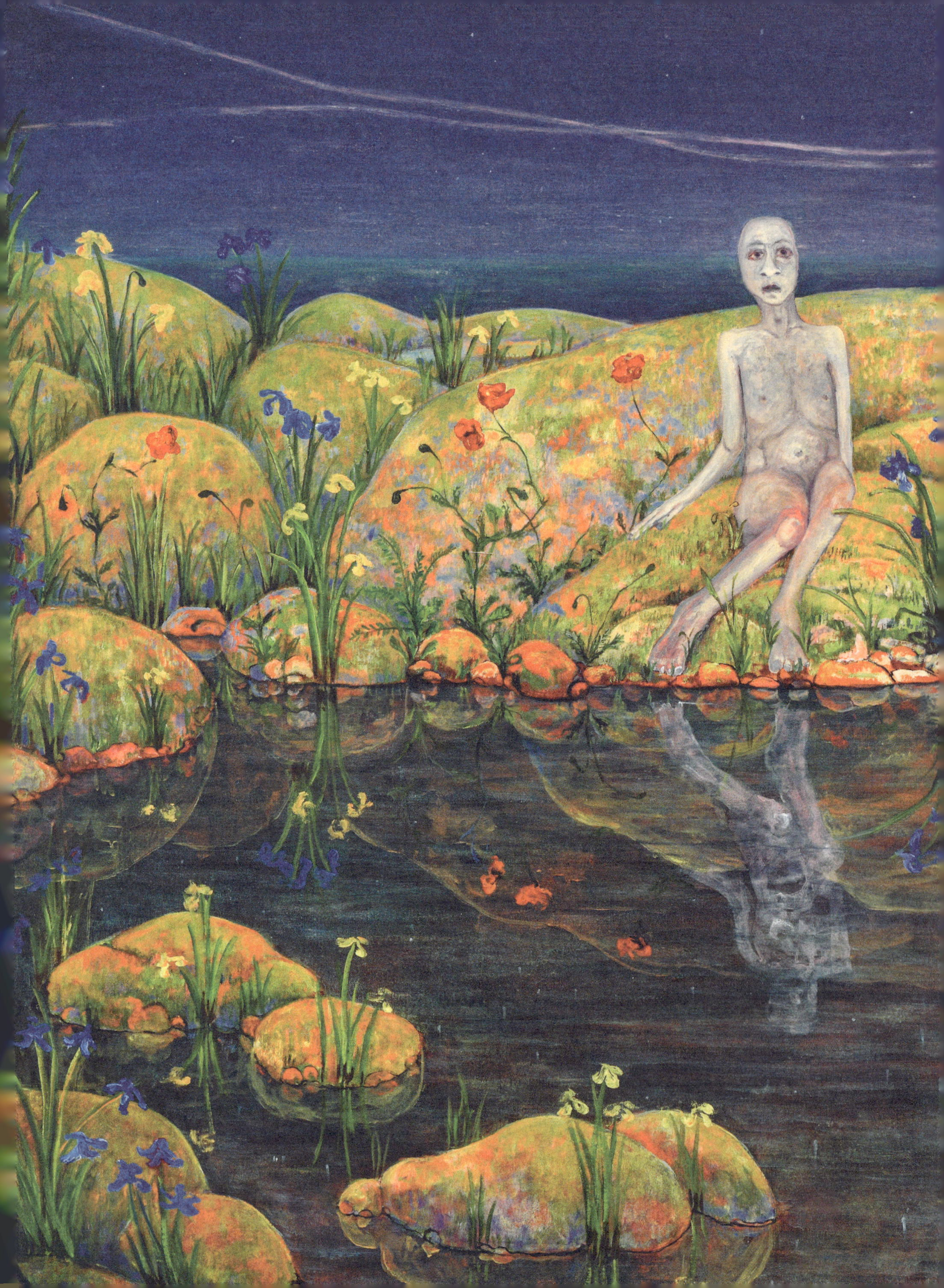

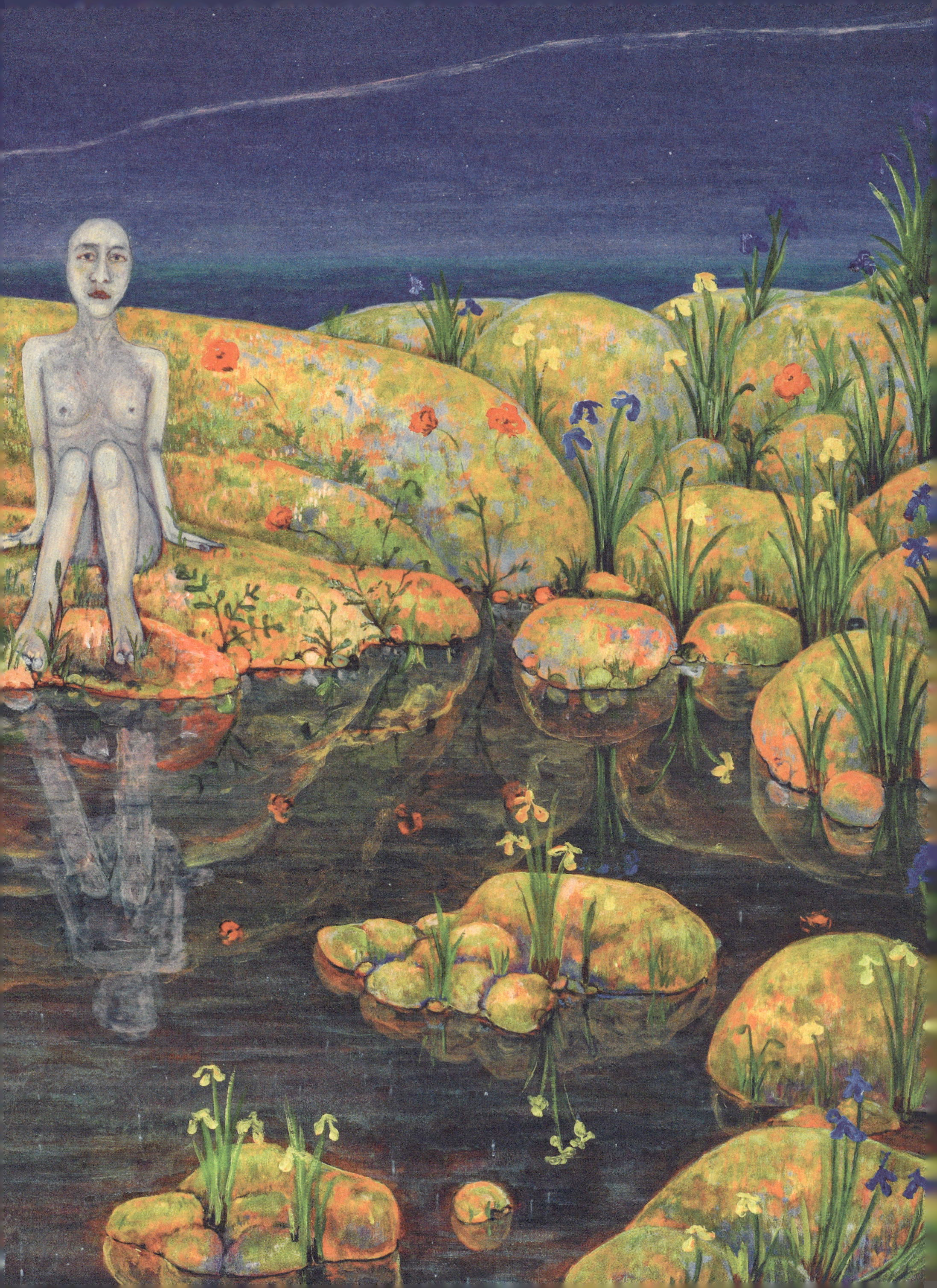

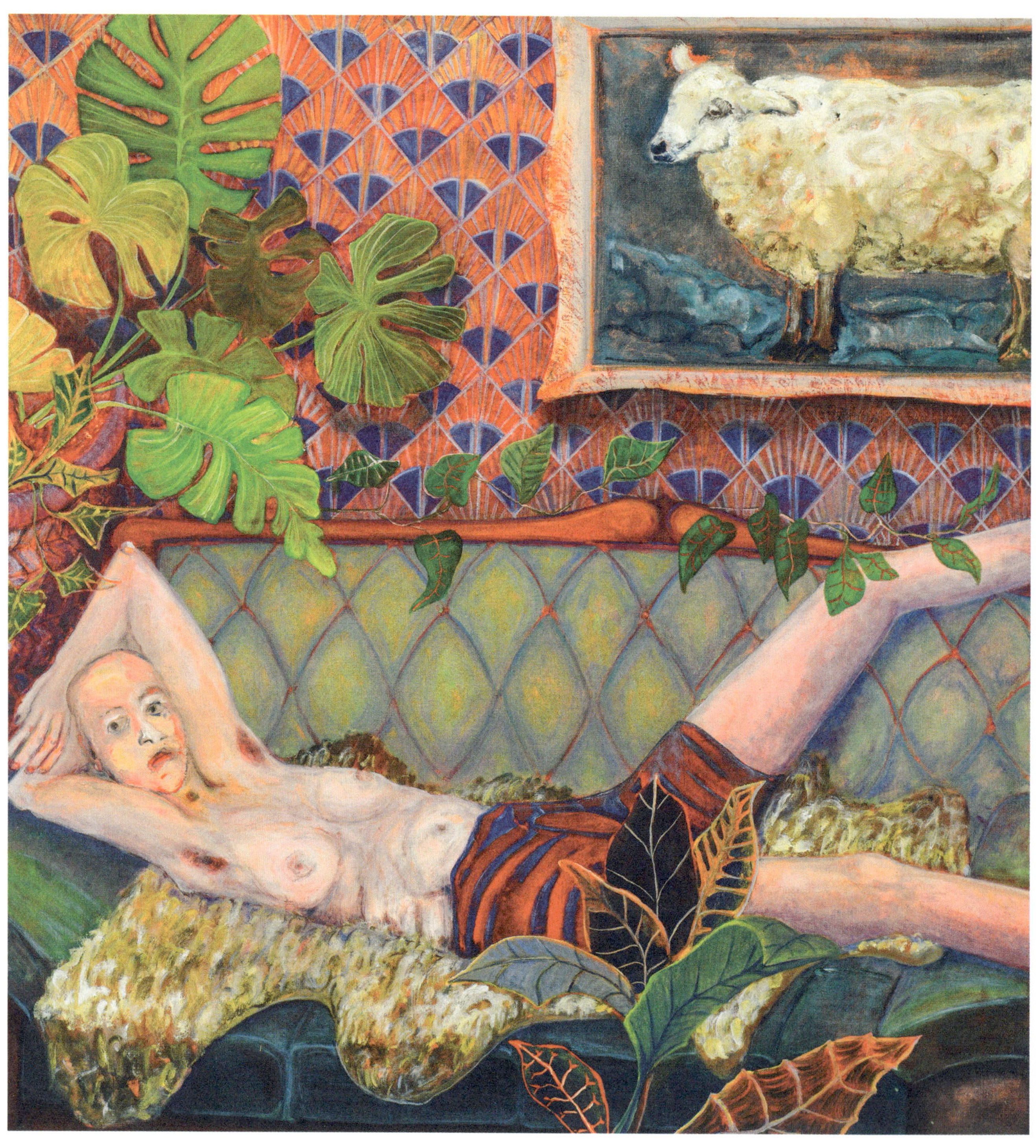

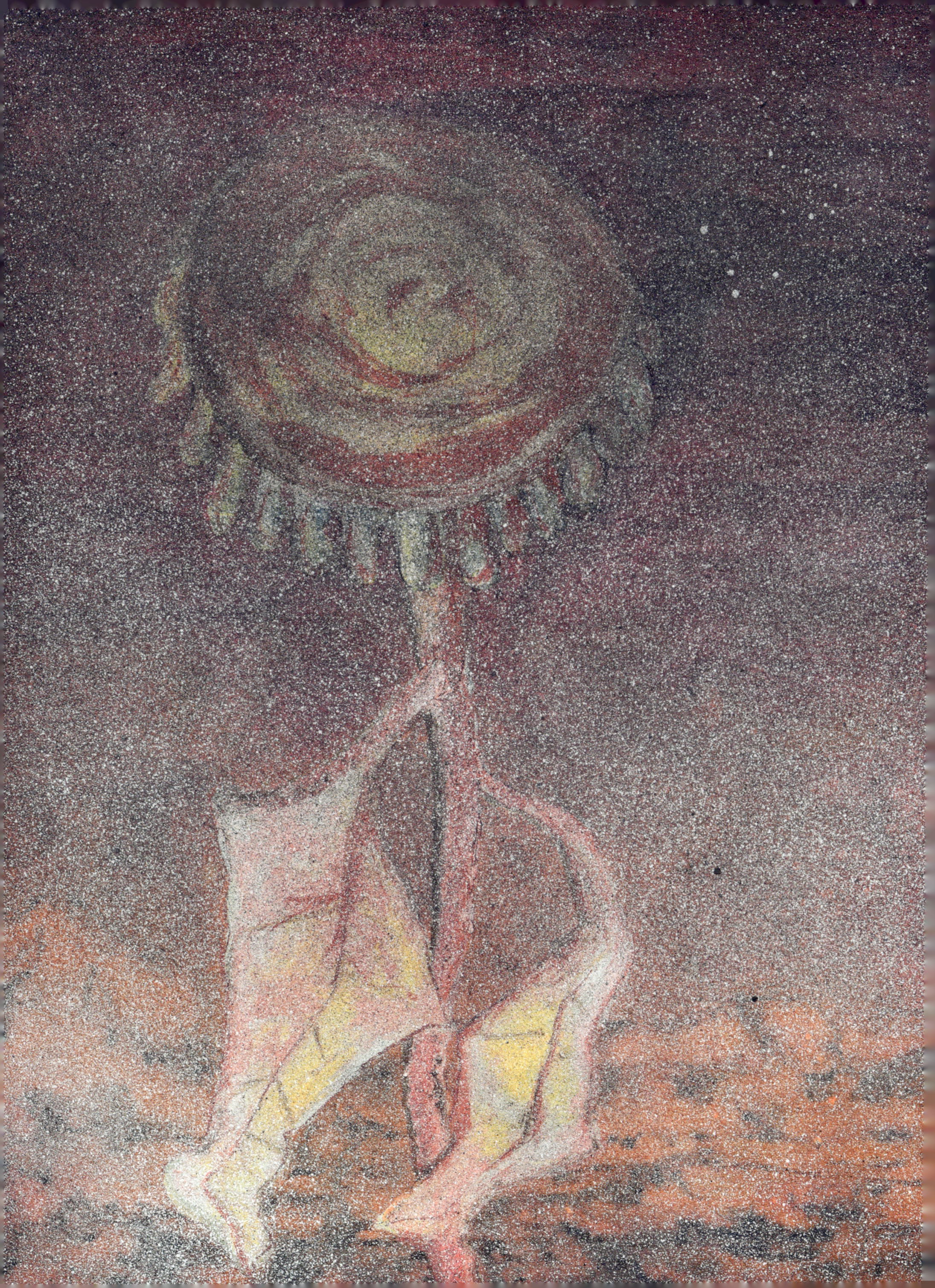

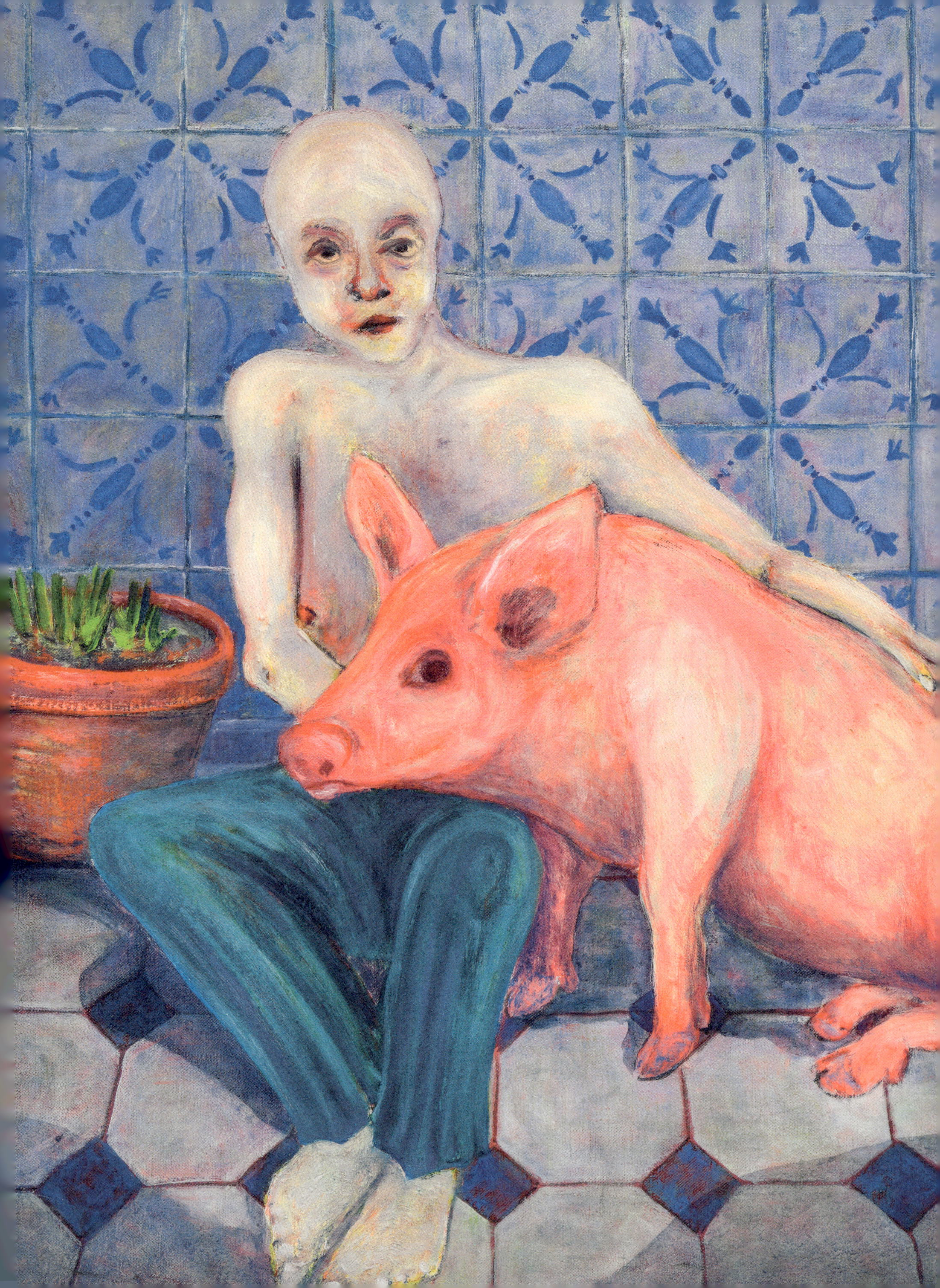

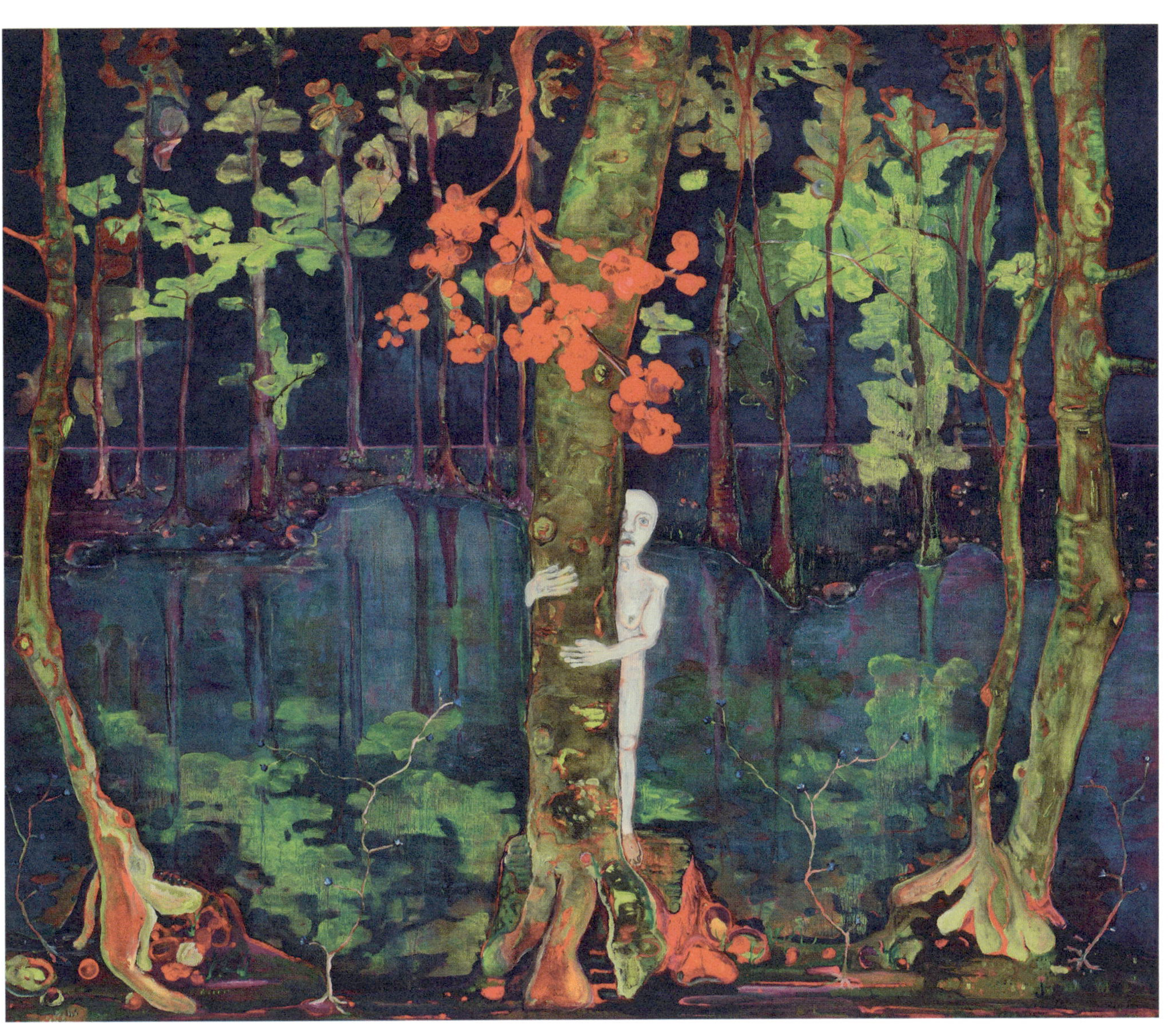

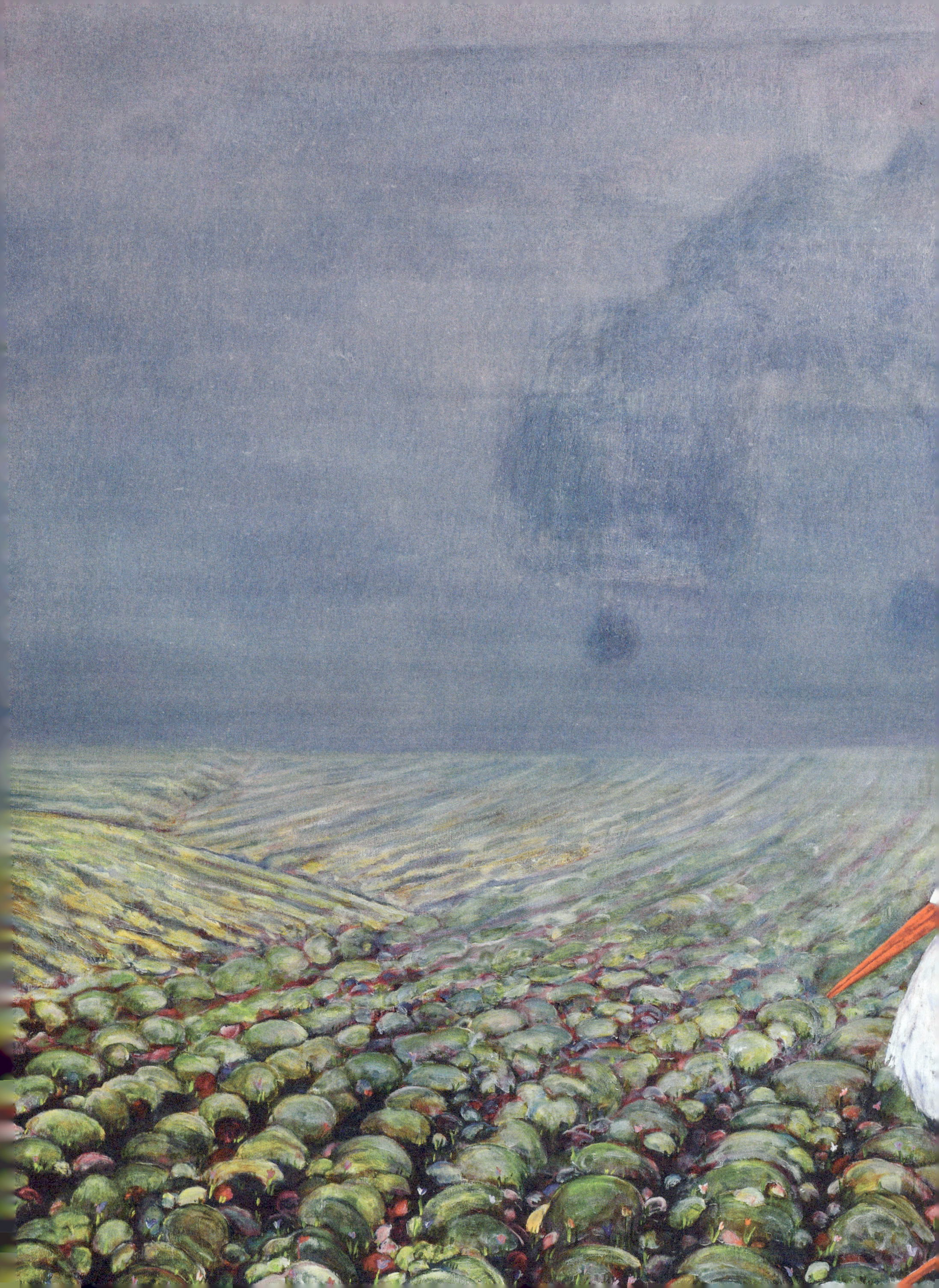

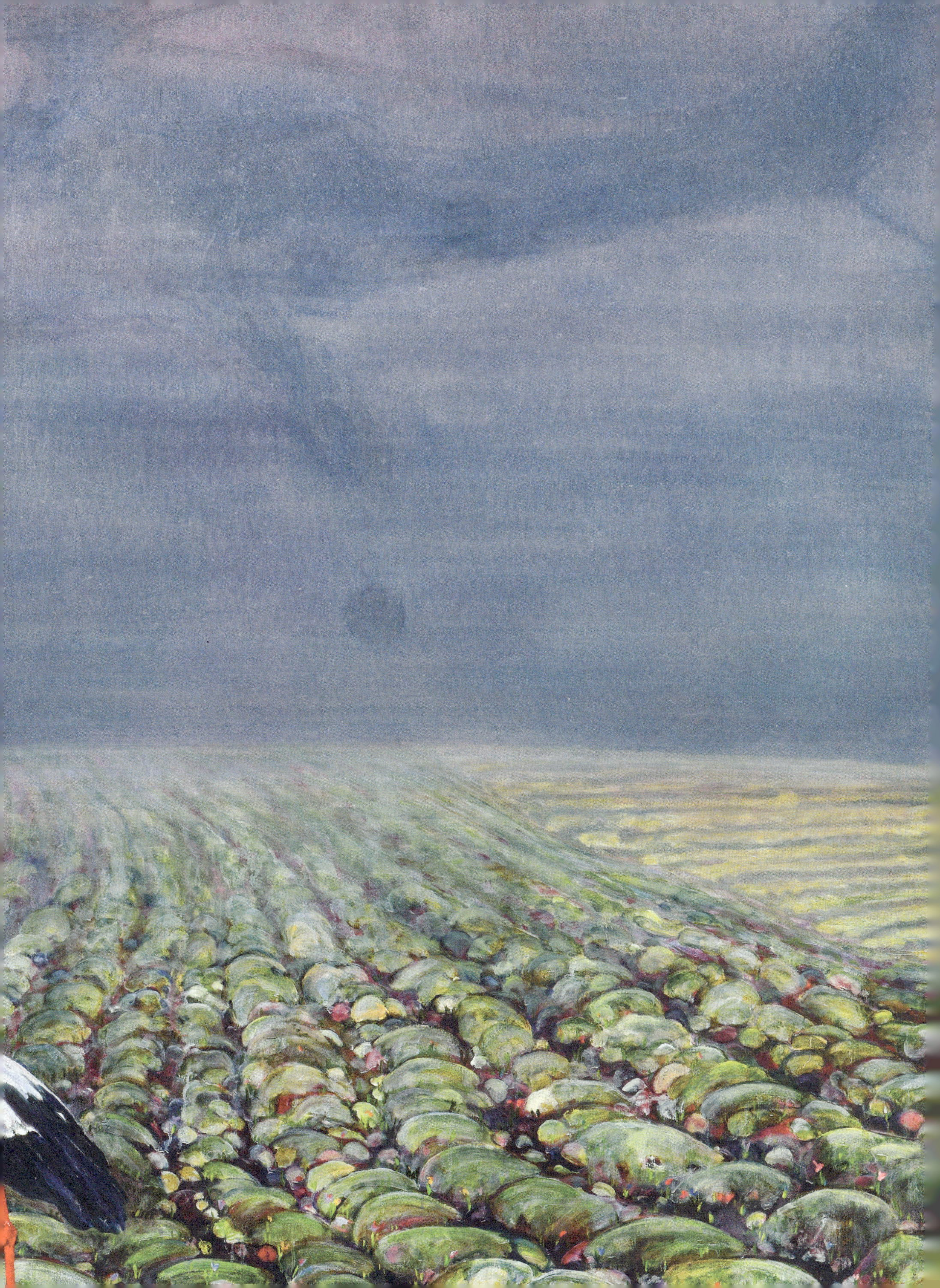

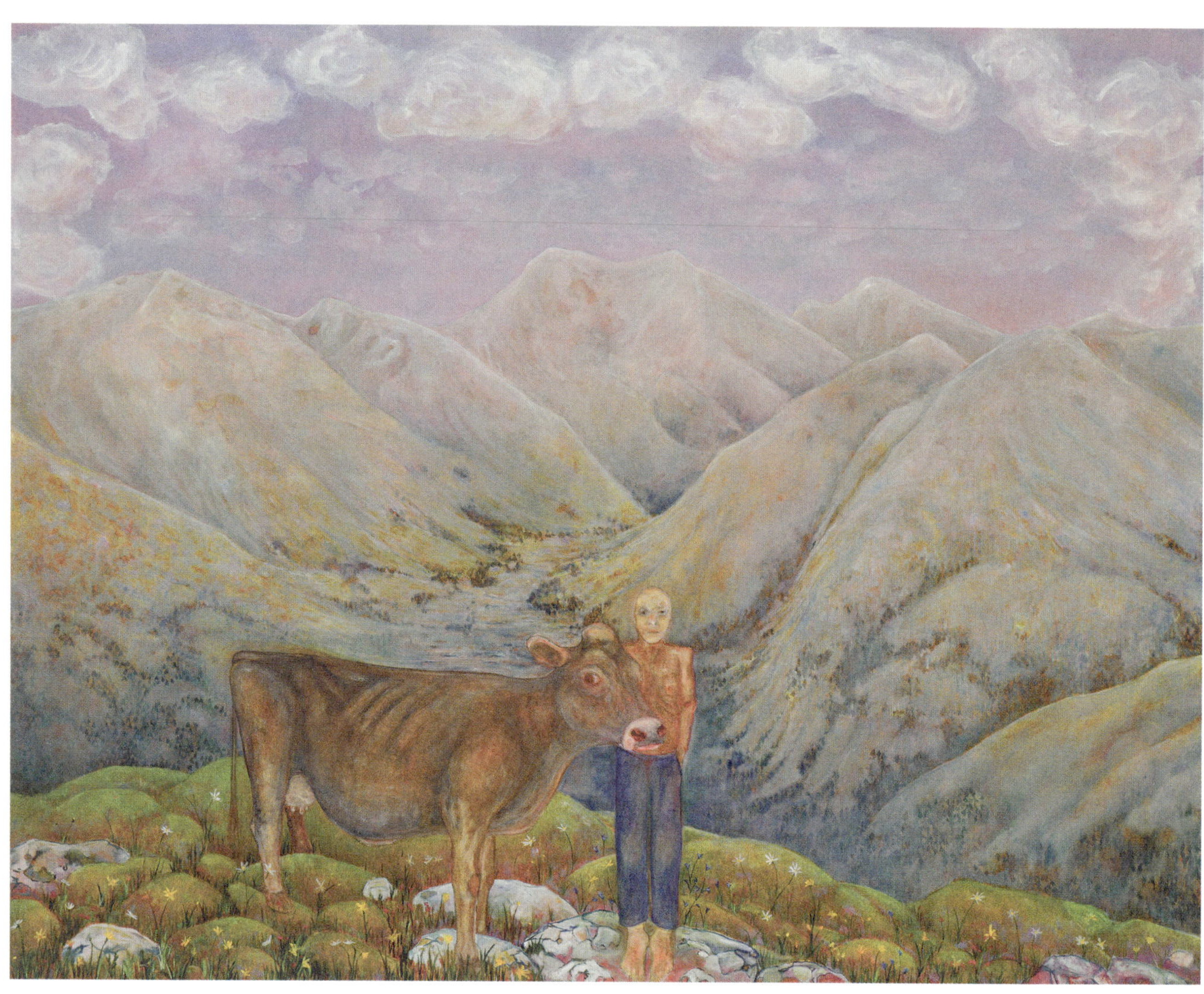

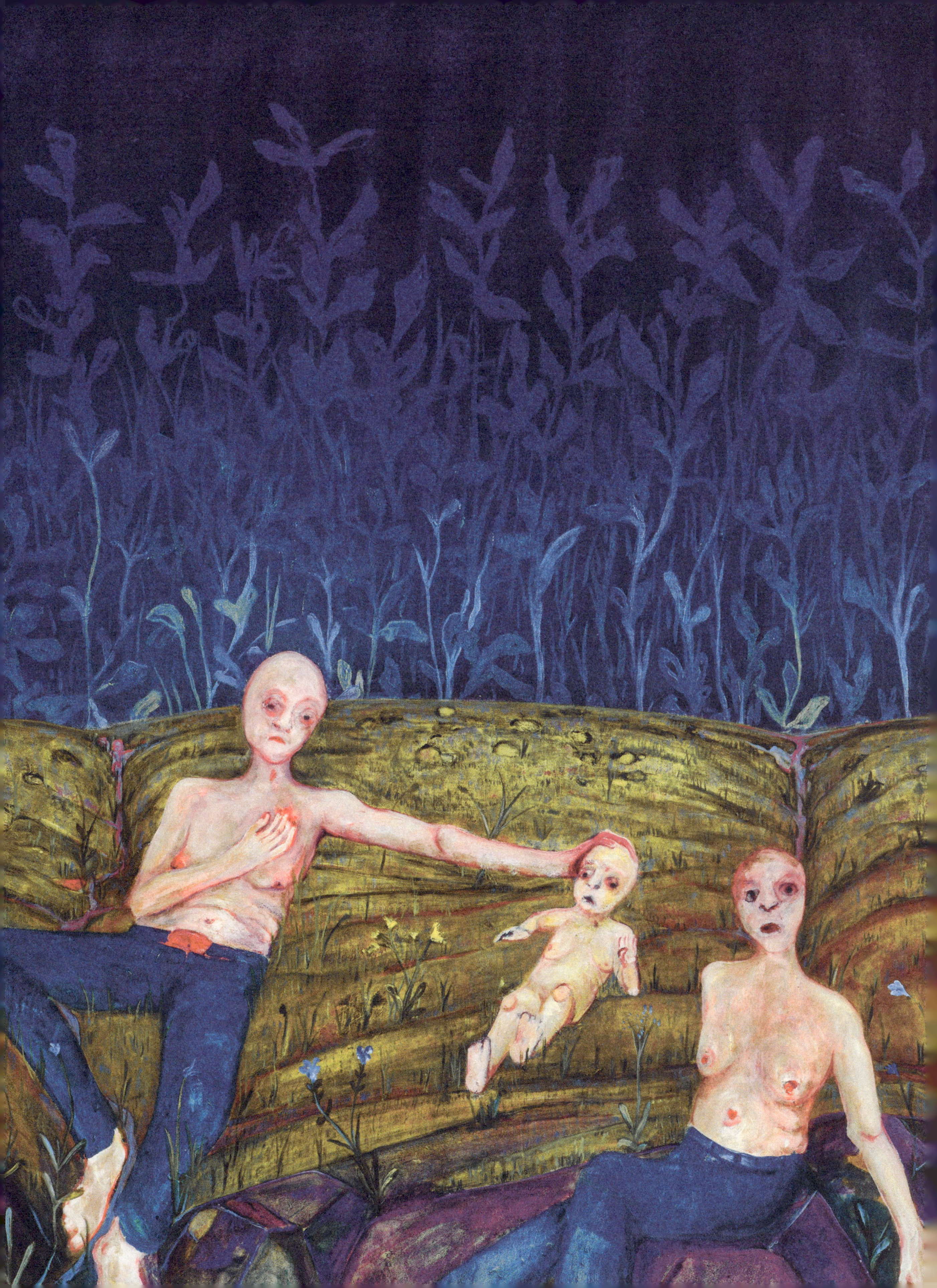

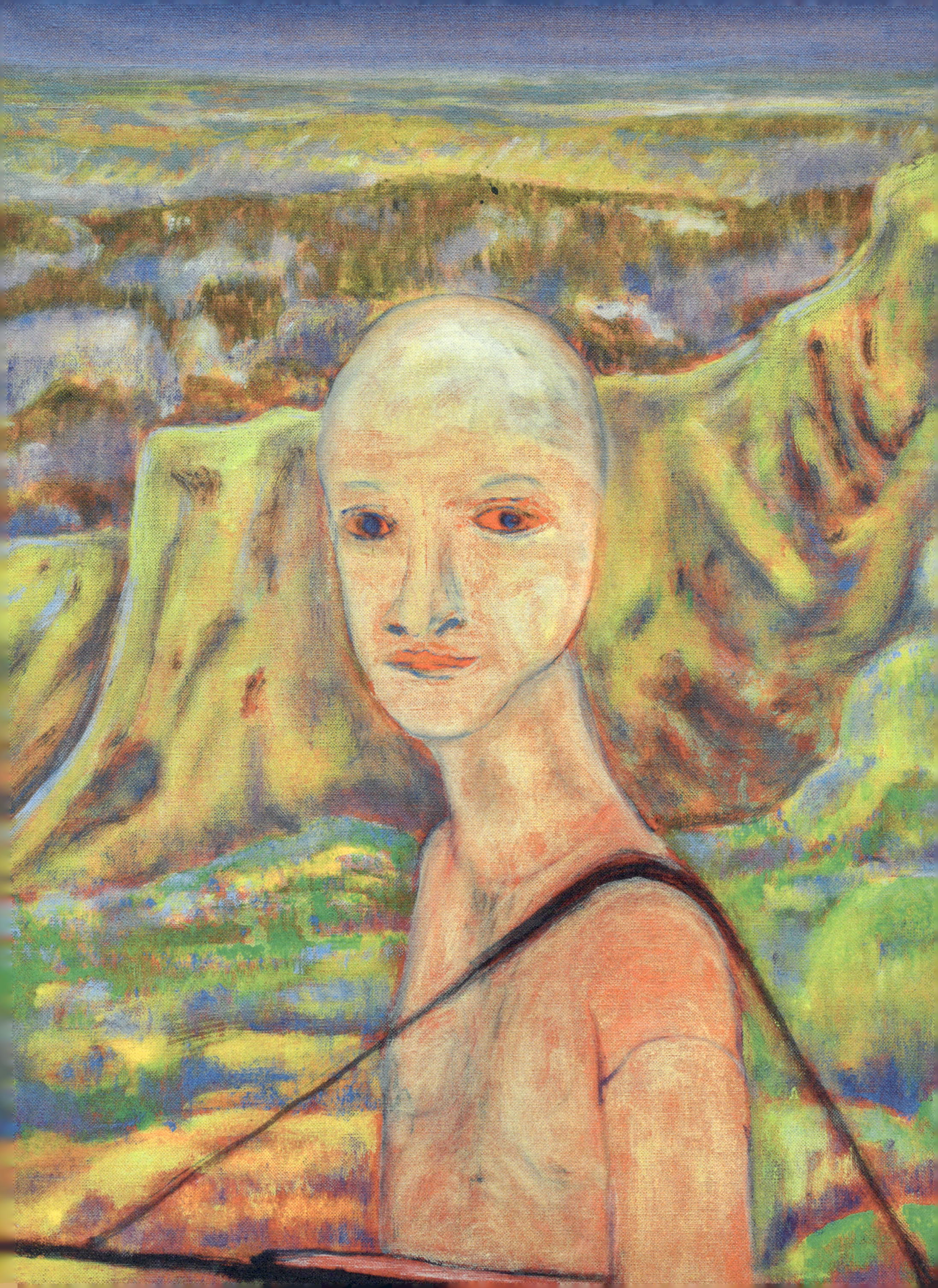

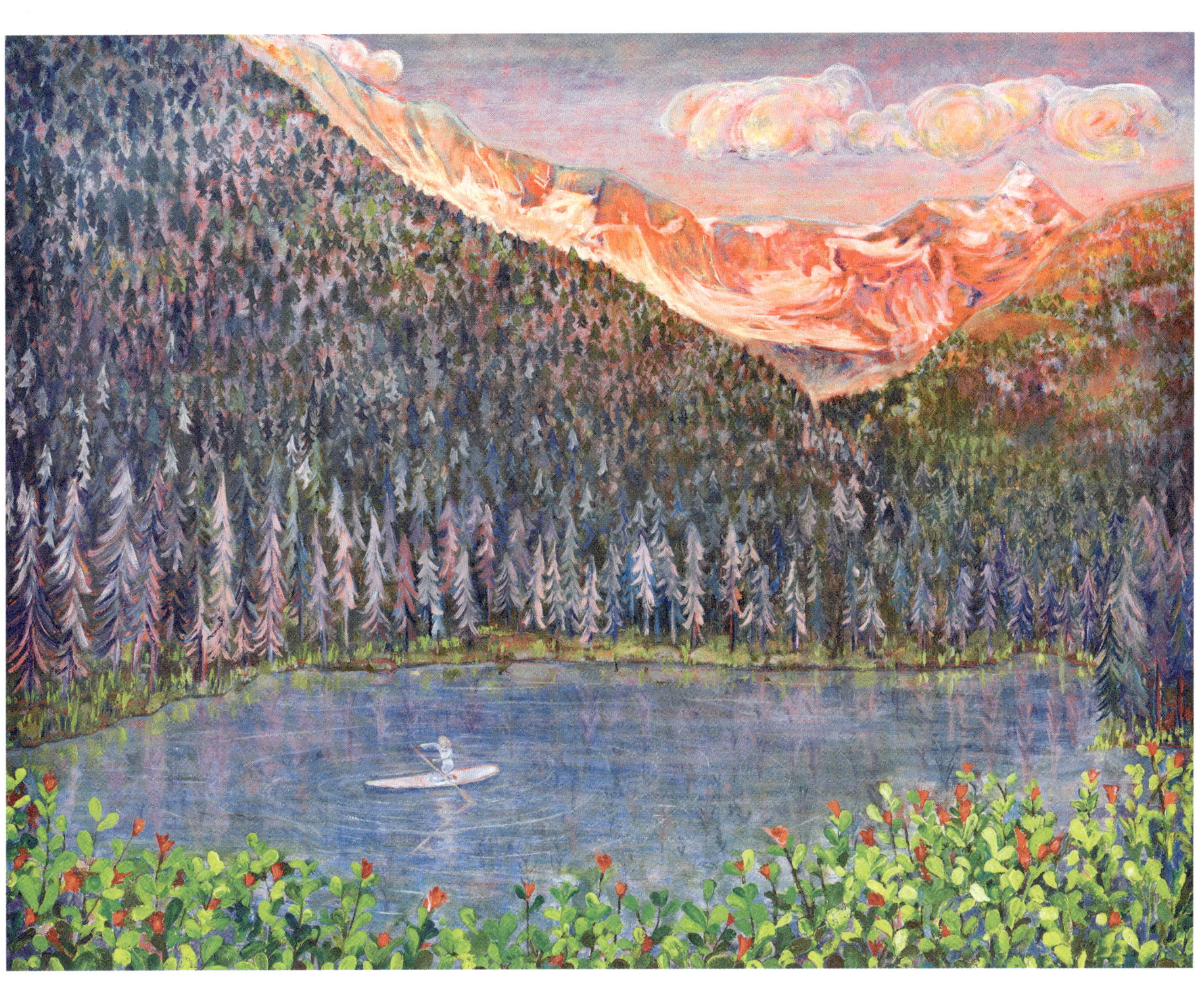

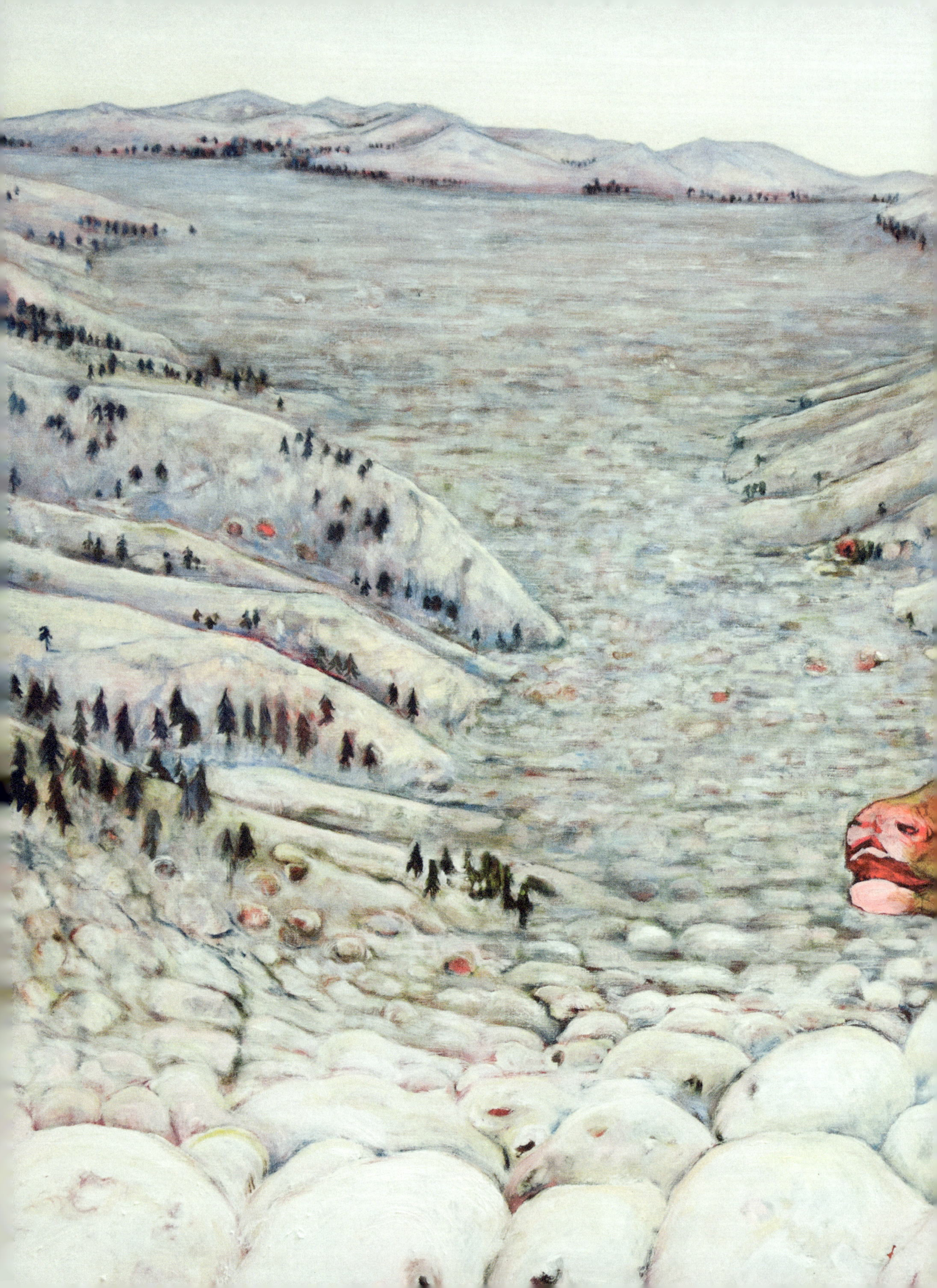

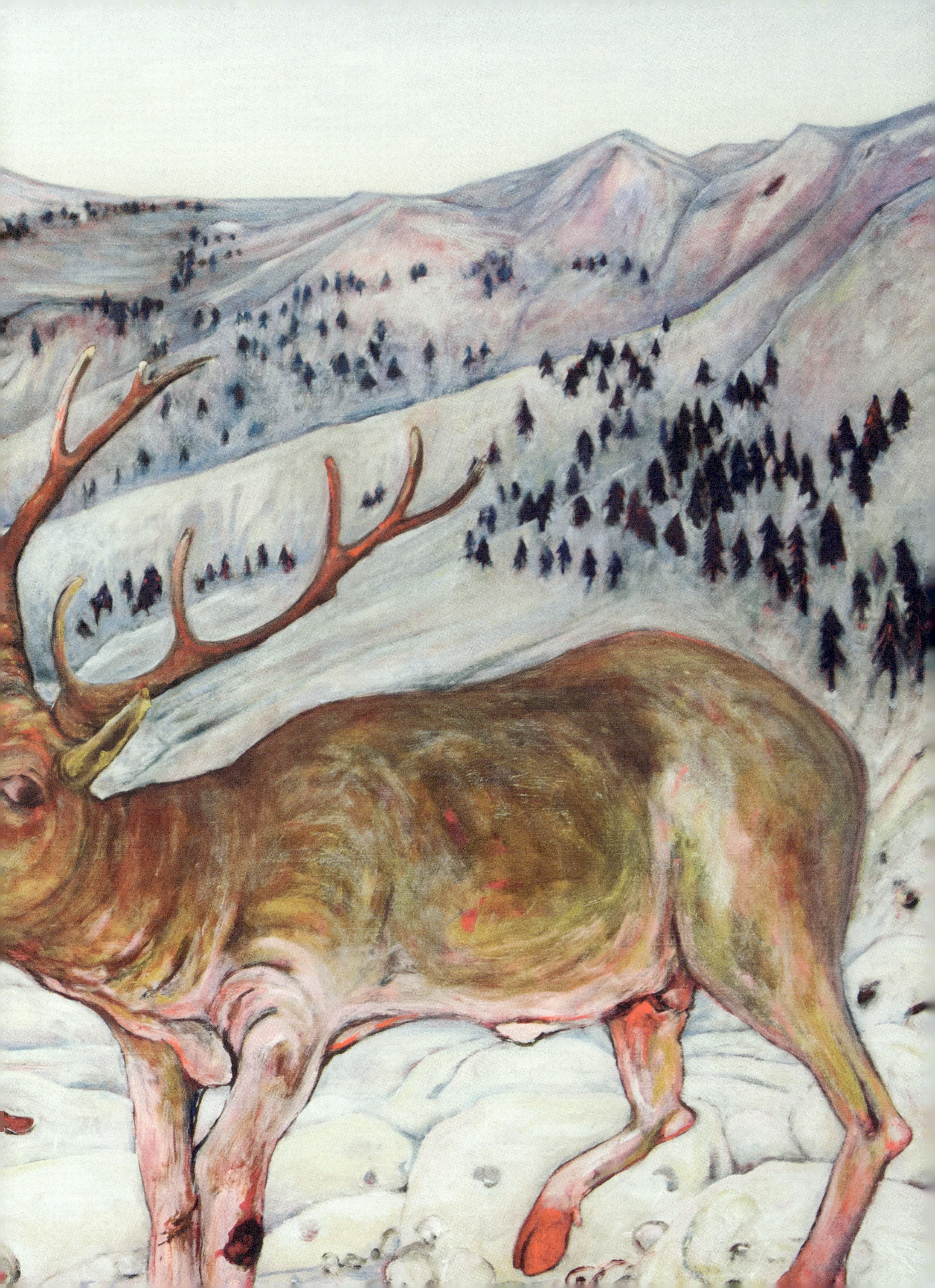

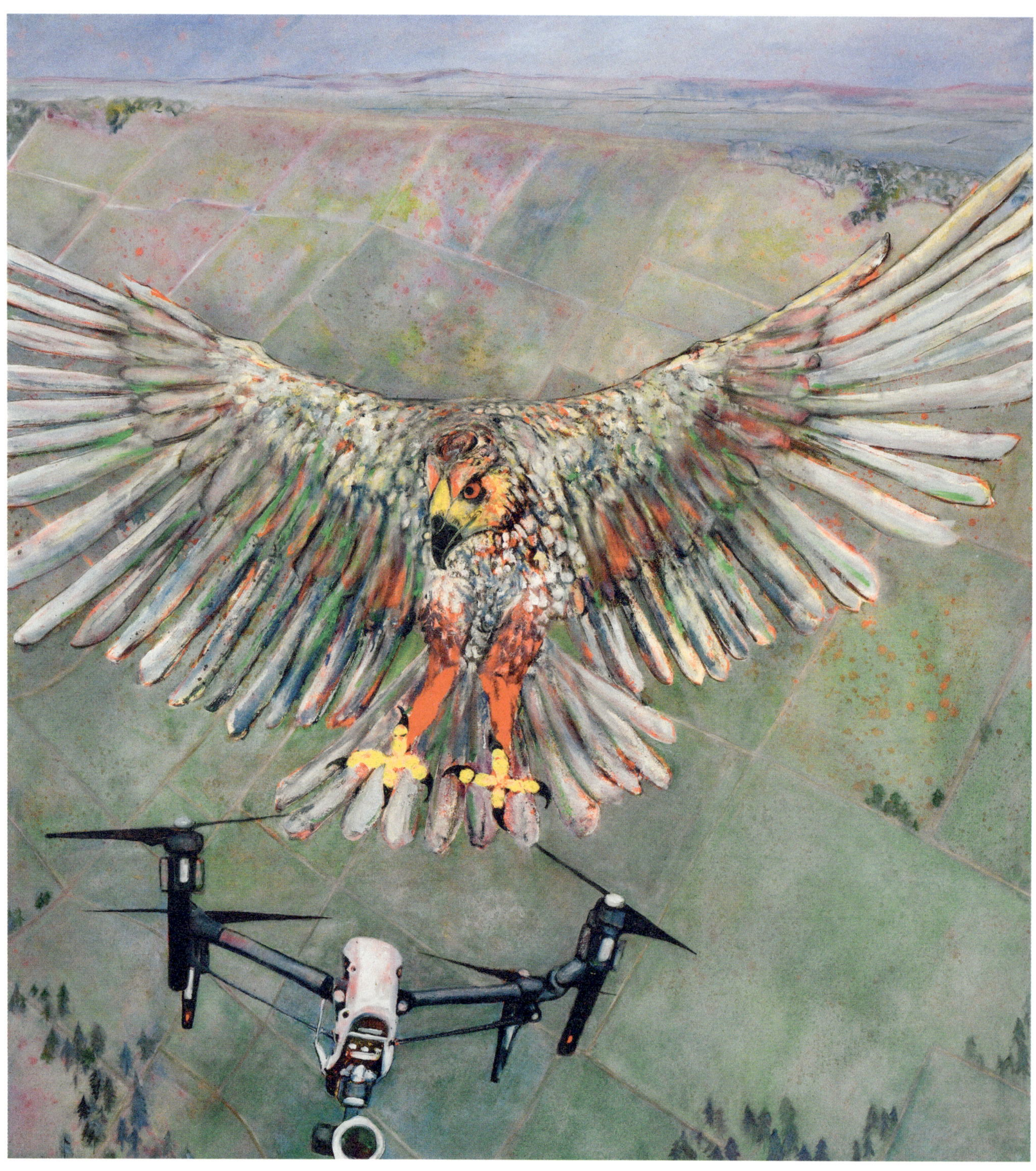

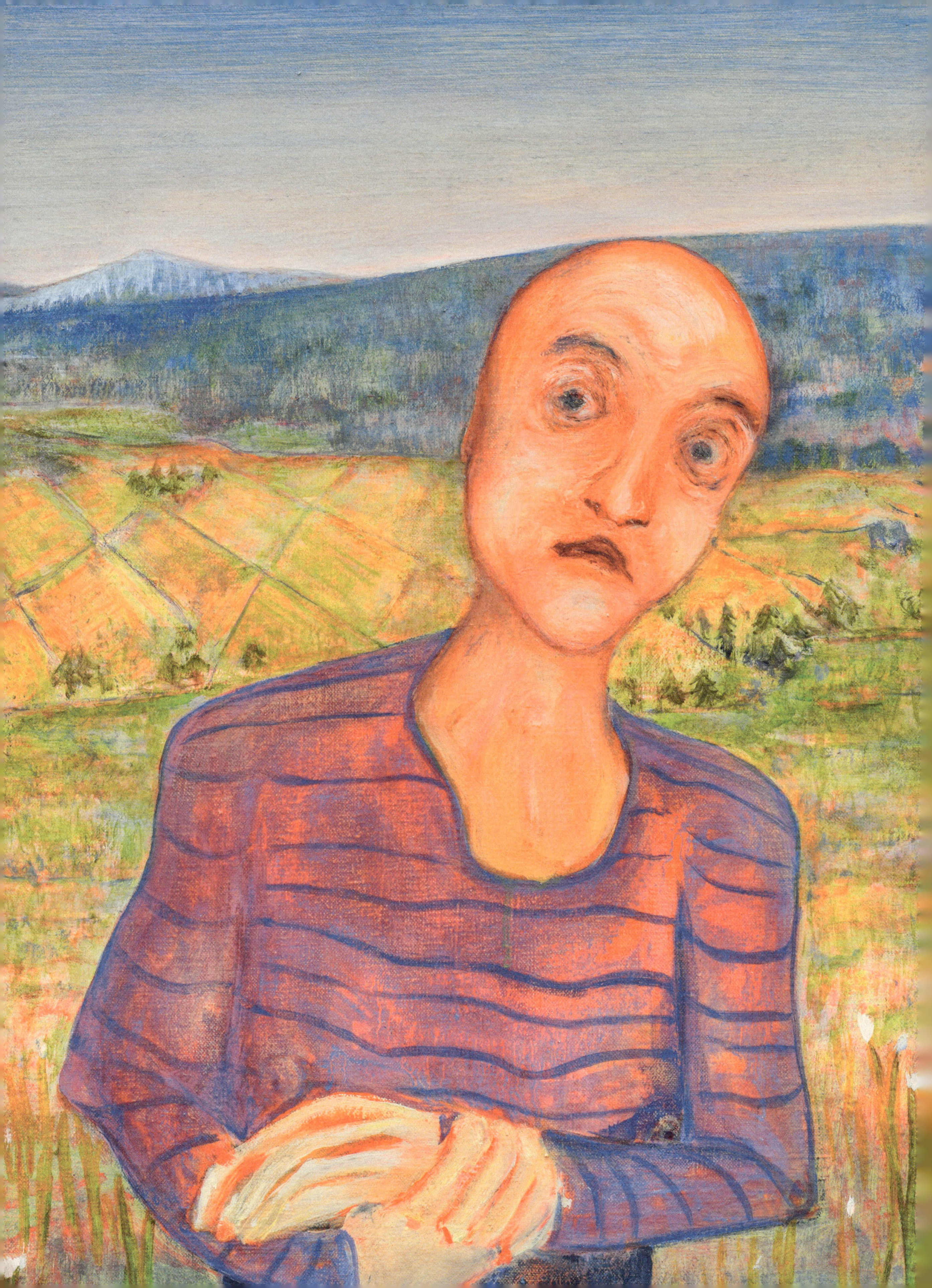

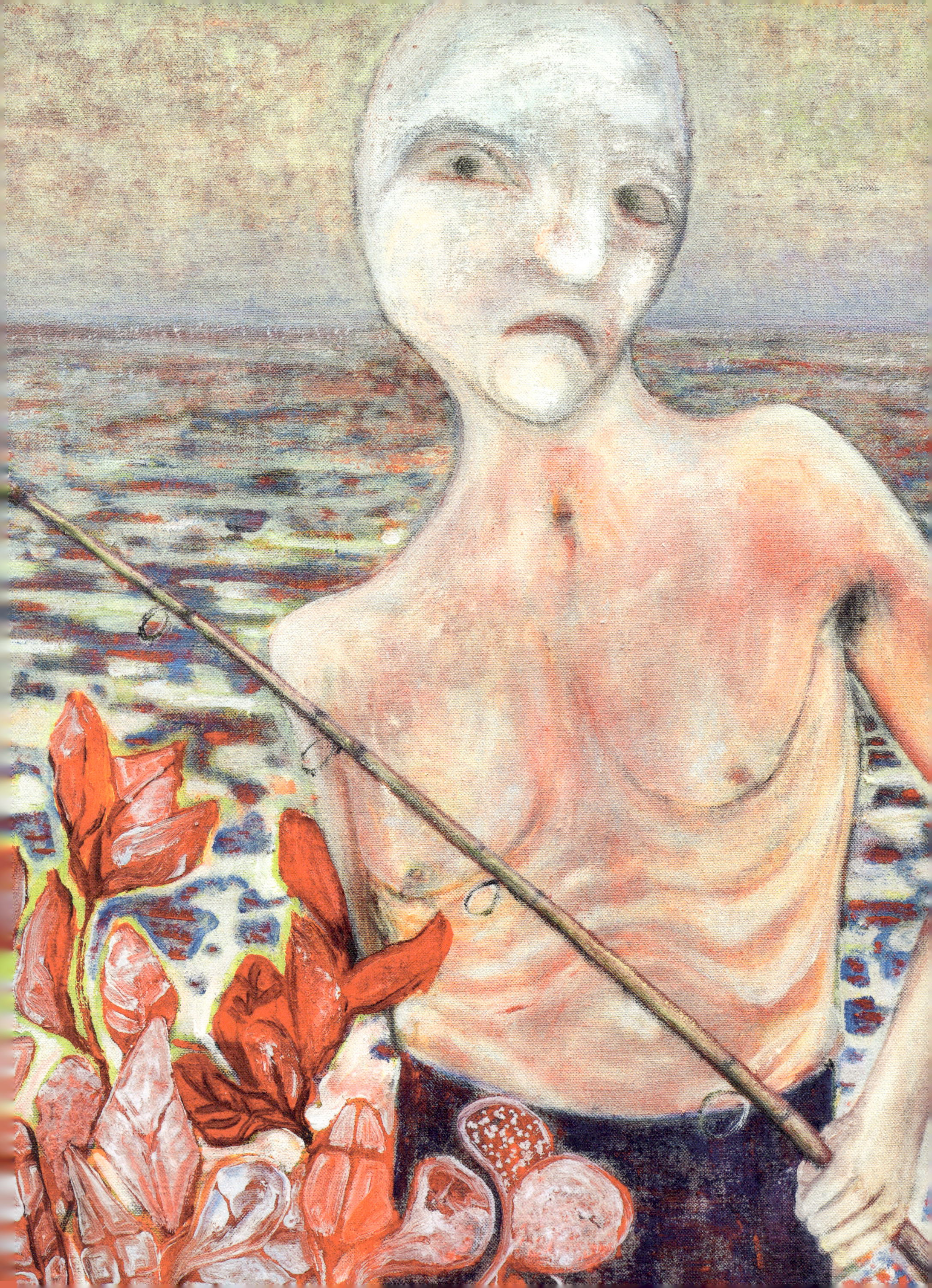

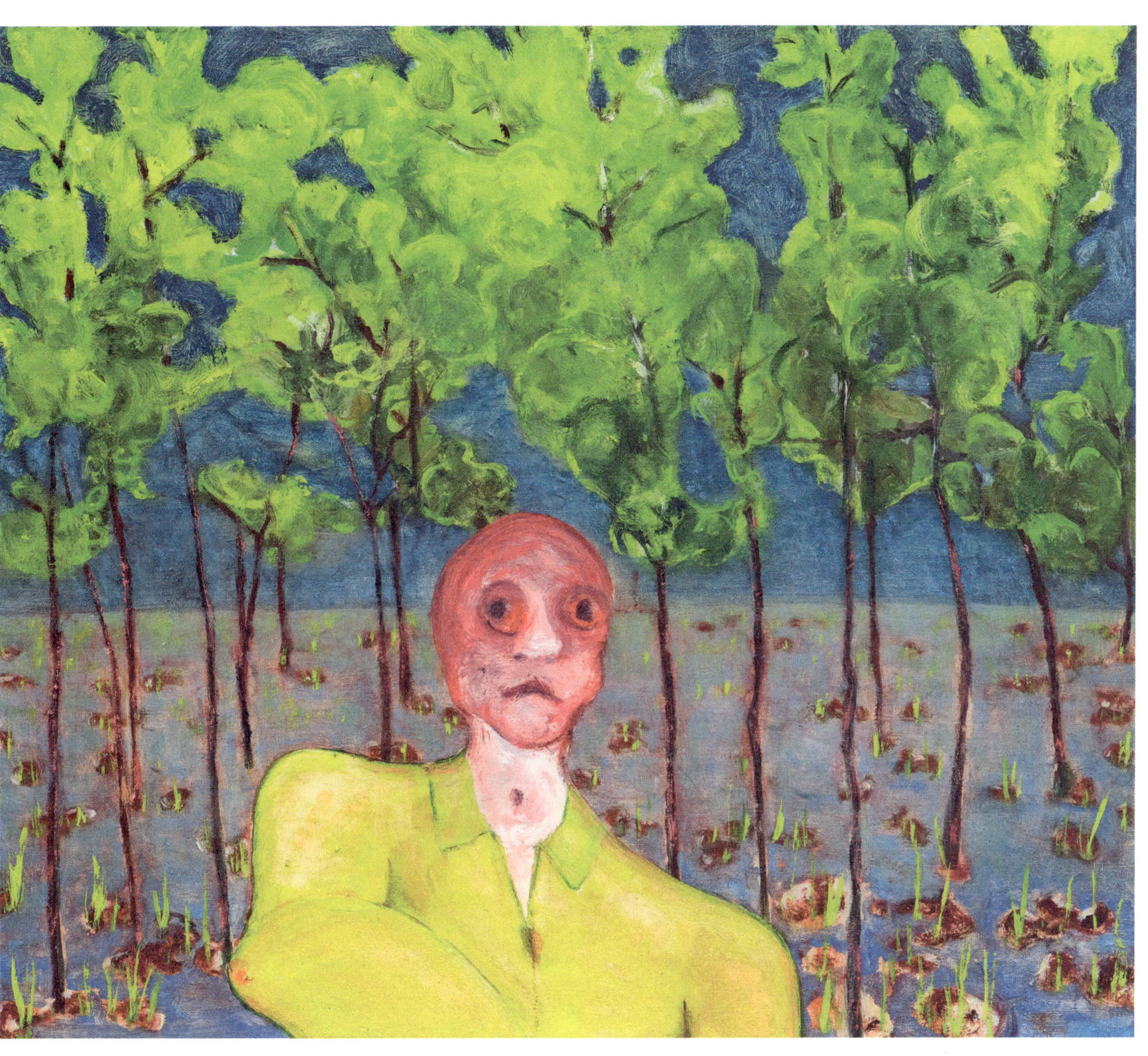

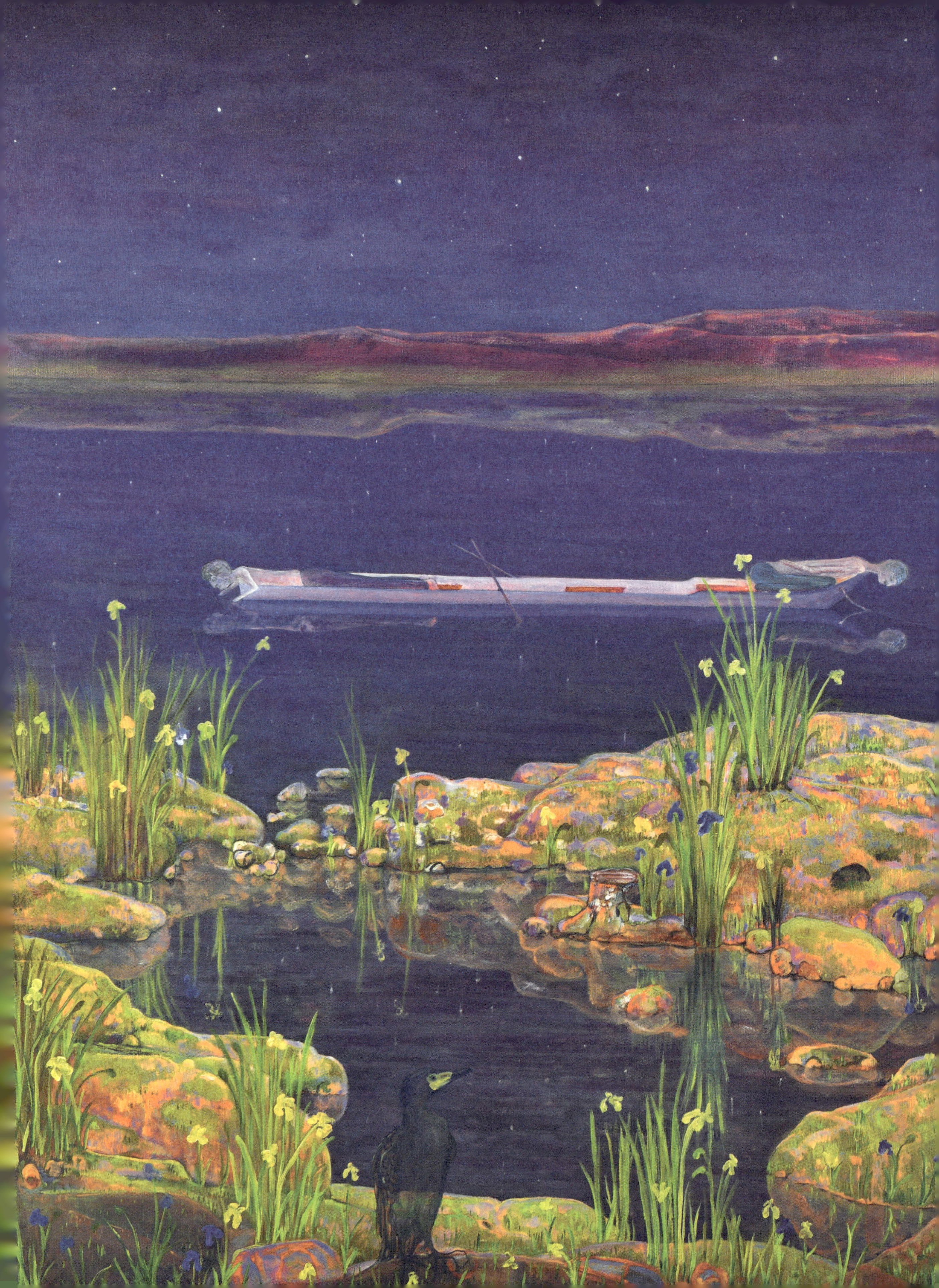

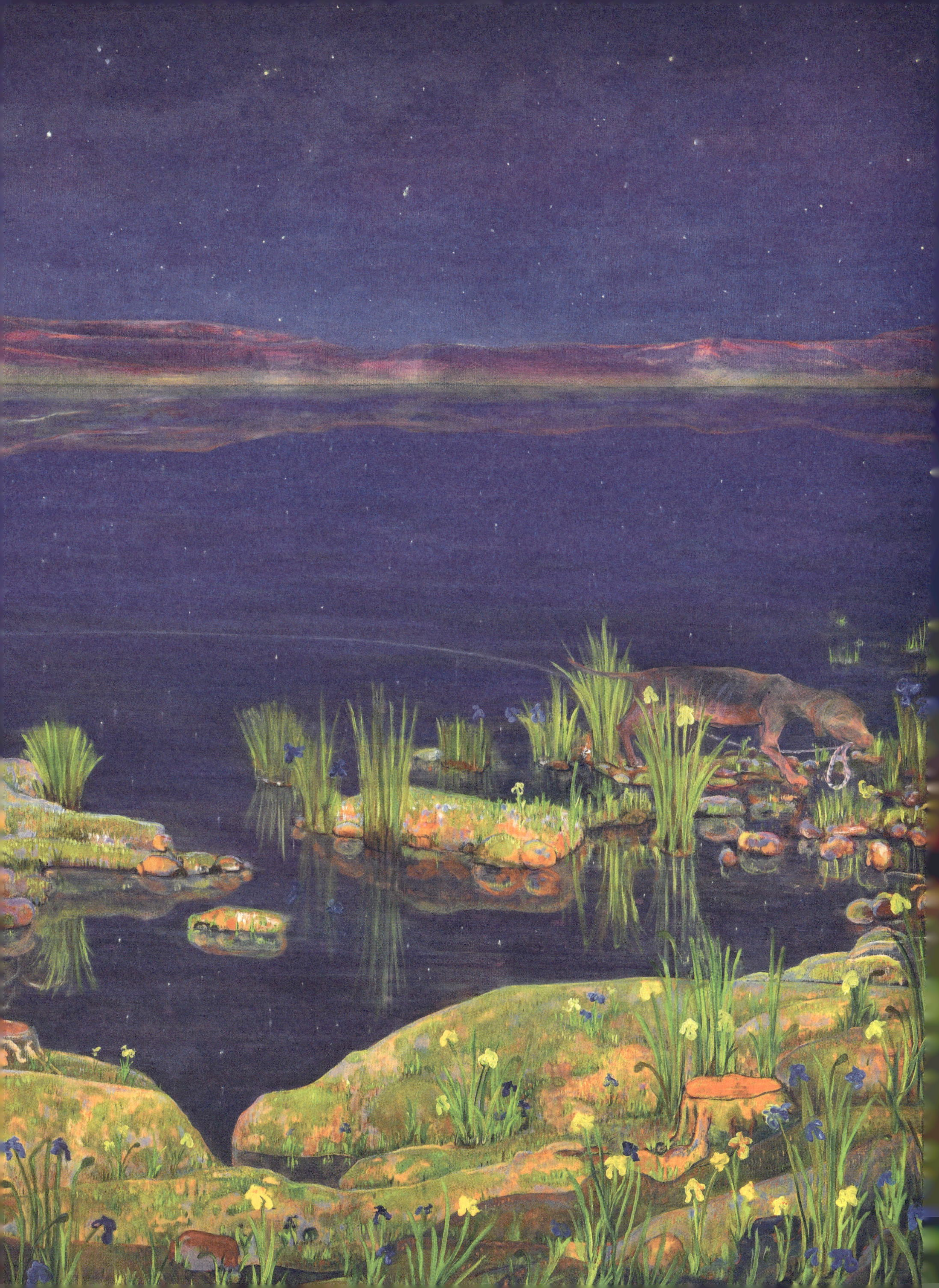

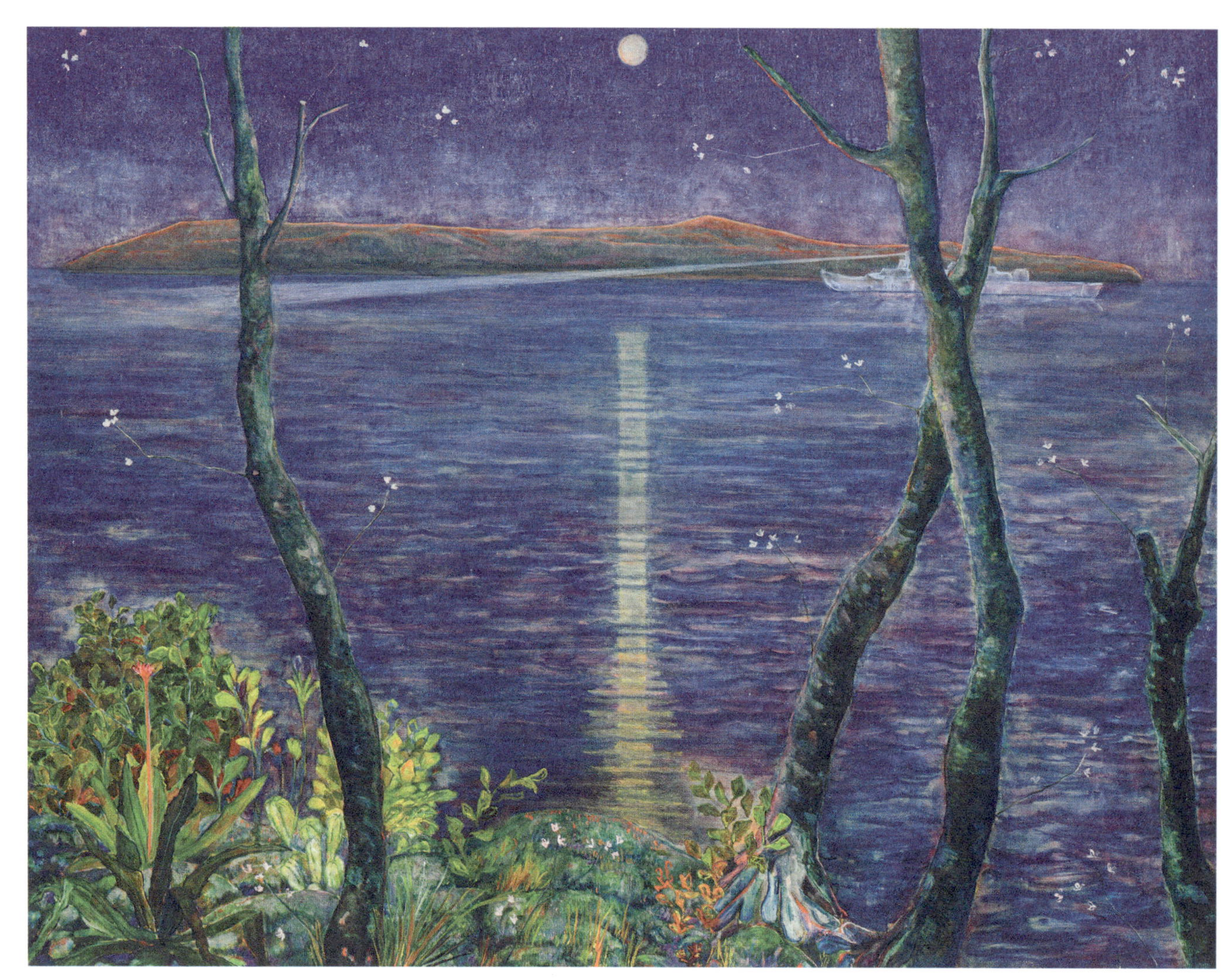

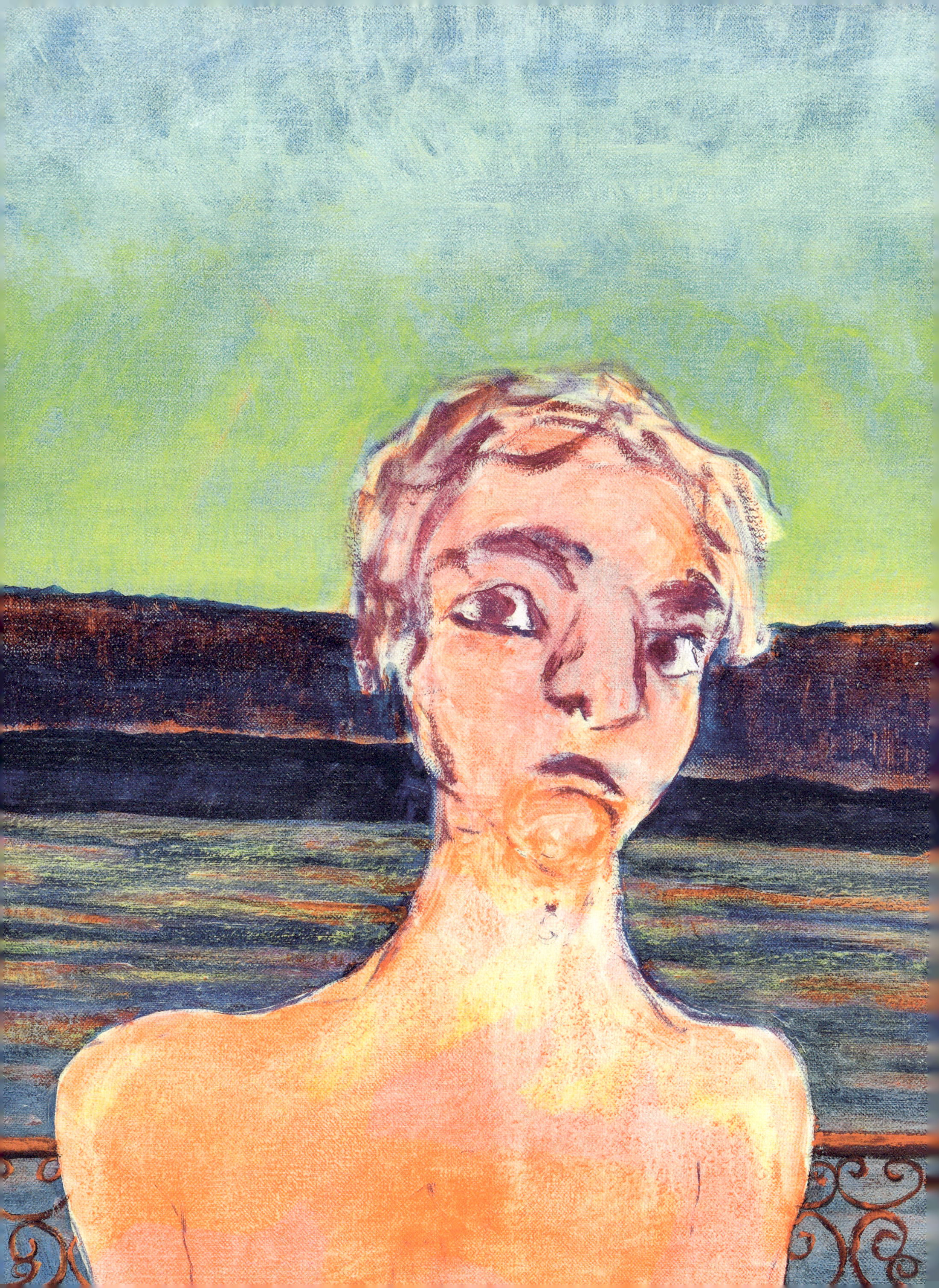

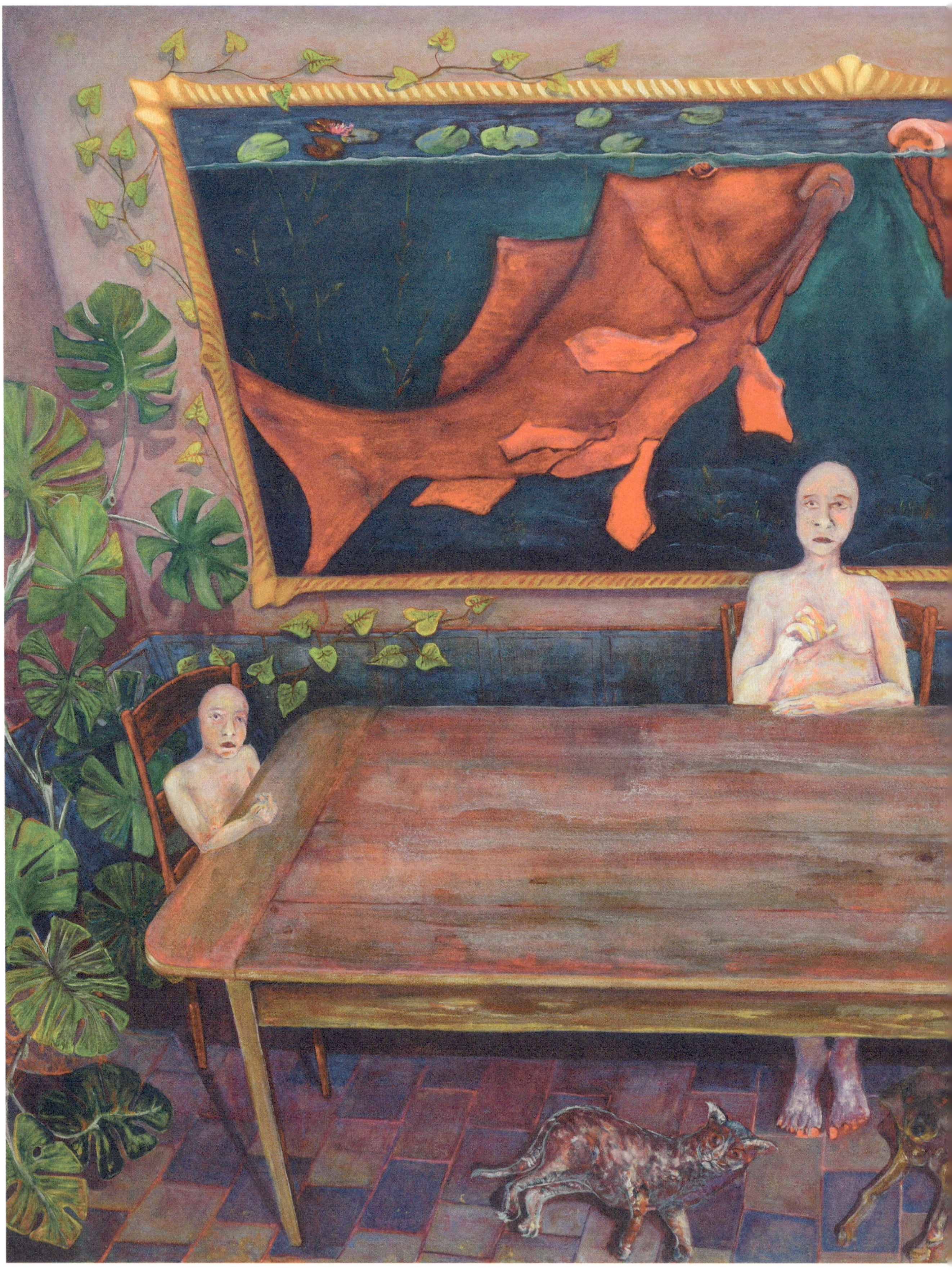

The moon is a perfect mirror
in which you can see nothing.

Adam Jasper

Leaf through the pages of the catalogue. What do you encounter? Rich landscapes, under the mauve tinted light of dusk or dawn. Animals, caught unexpectedly and eager to move. Wraith like figures, staring back at you. And finally, the hovering presence of those machines of war, drones and helicopters. What kind of world is represented here? Perhaps the best explanation needs to begin with a digression. Look away from the paintings, idle away some time with this text, and I will tell you something.

Andriu Deplazes' paintings, in ways that are not immediately obvious, have an affinity to Byzantine mosaics and Russian Orthodox Icon painting. Wherein lies this affinity? Well, in the case of a Byzantine mosaic, the artist always begins with the *eyes* of the central figure being portrayed, and spirals out from there. The eyes are where the primary power of the sacralised image resides. The size of the eyes and their distance from each other sets the measure for the rest of the composition. This process, halfway between ritual and technique, creates the mood that people casually attribute to such paintings: the transfixing outward gaze of the image. As a result, Byzantine mosaics and Orthodox icons are both some of the most charismatic and least realistic modes of portraiture that one can encounter. The figures in such images are usually centrally placed in a symmetrically arranged space, and they see you, rather than you seeing them. You come into *their* space, and receive their blessing (or curse), a phenomena that in Hindu contexts is called "darshan".

Now Deplazes' paintings don't immediately *resemble* orthodox icons. But thinking about the force of icons provides a point of anchorage in encountering his work. Very often, his nude, pale figures look directly out of the image, as if they were standing directly on the other side of a window and were peering into the space in which you stand. As if they saw something around you that you don't see yourself, and have good reason to be anxious about it. There is, to borrow a term from theatre, *no fourth wall* in these paintings. The image sees you. And the image sees you so forcefully that it takes quite a long time to fully register that the figures depicted are almost entirely without attributes. Much as ghosts, they are sexless, hairless, usually naked. For the moment, let's leave the jury out on whether these humanoid figures are people, or spirits. Their faces express human emotions, and their gestures are familiar, but their bodies seem almost prisons, both unsuited to the landscape, and yet almost like landscapes in and of themselves, with their paunchy imperfection. Let's call these figures "avatars".

What kind of spaces do these avatars inhabit? Usually, landscapes of outrageous beauty. Alpine spaces of hallucinatory force, influenced by Ferdinand Hodler and Félix Vallotton, or overflowing with exuberant vegetation, like one of Henri Rousseau's jungles. They are the paradises of dreams, the abundant spaces that flip between generosity to the spirit, and hostility to civilisation. Within these landscapes animals—whether quadrupeds or birds—carry the same intelligence and autonomy of the avatars, but they seem somewhat better adapted. They are part of the world that they inhabit, rather than haunting it, or haunted by it.

Deer and white vastness (2020), In the foreground is a deer, so close to the viewer that it appears as if it might be able to step from the picture into the room. In the background, there is a Hodler-inspired landscape of auratic snow-covered mountains bathed in the pink light of a sunset. The content and the title of the image would, at first glance, seem almost provocatively conservative: deer, snow field, mountain. Except that the world is just a little out of joint. Deplazes is a sensitive colourist, and the colours in this painting seep anxiety. The horizon is literally askew, as if we are looking at a painting based on a photo taken with an unsteadily held camera. And the deer, well, its flesh has the tone of a naked mole rat that has spent its life in the lab, not the gamey muscle you'd expect of an animal that has lived its life in the wild. Its eyes are swivelled back with alarm, and it appears to be trying to frantically reverse away from the shock of who it sees in the gallery, as if you look worse than it does. It's as if the protagonists of the *Geistige Landesverteidigung* got a prophetic vision of the contemporary Swiss scene and, well, freaked out.

Deplazes' backgrounds are where he shows his facility as a painter. He appropriates, and executes (in both senses of the word) the early twentieth century conventions for representing idealised Swiss landscapes. But what kind of landscape does the painter inhabit? Deplazes, like most contemporary painters, maintains a studio rather than working in the open air, and his studio has moved several times, from Zurich, to Brussels, to Marseilles, where he now spends much of his time. In Brussels, Andriu Deplazes praised the cosmopolitan black humour, but alpine landscapes appeared more prominently in his paintings after he moved his studio to Marseilles: as if two steps of removal were needed in order for the artist to fully embrace both the extraordinary beauty of the Swiss landscape, and everything about its representation that is so alienating, so oppressive, so *owned* by the institutions that determine identity and membership.

The avatars present a riddle. One could understand their dilemma as an existential one, but if so, it is existentialism as we have it from Albert Camus, it is haunted by pure absurdity. The palpable sense that humans are the animal that is both unfit to live, and yet refuses to die, because it does not know how. An animal that hides itself in the most absurd camouflages, such as the disguise of prestige. That seeks refuge in dominating its own kind. Even though the figures are stripped of individual attributes, they show the result of these dynamics well. There is a particular kind of therapy called "family constellations," or *Familienaufstellung*, in German. Within it, people, or even objects, can take the positions of family members. And through role play, dynamics within the family, whether of domination, submission or provocation, can reveal themselves.

As an example, take the new painting *Bodies at table* (2021). It shows an adult figure at a large table, flanked by two children, left and right. Below the table are two pets, a dog and a cat, also looking directly out of the image. The central figure dominates the space of the table. They are, to use a slightly obnoxious phrase, clearly the "head of the household". And this is also clearly a prosperous house. In the background are flourishing *monstera* and ornamental creeping vines. But what absolutely dominates the space is a painting within a painting, two enormous koi carp, the colour of rust, colliding with each other. The waterline in the painting on the back wall is set above all the figures in the room, and one cannot help but feel, looking at this image, as if one has entered a completely airless space, as if the figures are drowning. And all of them look at you as if perturbed, as if you have intruded upon something, as if you have interrupted them in a ritual, and now they expect something of you.

But who are you? Are you yourself, or another avatar, or something else again? In this image, the angle of view is too high for you to be a figure of the same scale as those that are seated. Did you fly in? The high angle suggests the third part of Deplazes practice, between landscape and human—and alludes to what are perhaps the most troubling of all of his protagonists. Drones and helicopters repeatedly appear within these paintings. They appear explicitly, or they are in the paintings as shadows, almost as watermarks, as toys, or are implied by the angle of view, the awkward "drone shot" that is not a conventional bird's eye view, and at the same time far removed from any human perspective. The drones are avenging angels, the coming of the holy spirit, enemies of all that is natural, and perhaps also a kind of radical evil. They are also sometimes you. When the framing of the image is from the drone's point of view, the position of the drone, and of the visitor to the gallery, collapses into one.

The drones also open a new potential space. Where previously there were two spaces: the space depicted within the painting, and the space of the room in which the painting hangs, in which you are standing as you look at it, a space that Deplazes' figures peer directly into, in violation of the principle of the fourth wall, there is a third, imagined space of surveillance— this is a complex game—the unknown screen to which this drone footage is transmitted. This third view is sometimes represented, sometimes only implied. And this brings us to the question that I can't answer, that I don't want to answer. Who is haunting whom? Are we haunted by landscapes, and by figures that imply the roles of domination and submission that characterise even normal families? Or are we haunting them? Are we pursued by drones, by mechanical eyes, or are the mechanical eyes ours? Like a nightmare that we've chosen to linger in, we find ourselves switching between the perspectives of the pursuer and the pursued. Painting was always a cultivated pursuit, but it was not intended to end like this, in an inescapable triangular trap created by viewer, subject and mechanical eye.

If there is a potential truce in the psychic and social conflicts suggested by the paintings, it can be seen in another painting, *Body and pig sitting* (2021). A younger figure, uncharacteristically wearing pants, sits against a cool wall of white and blue tiles. A terracotta pot on one side, and a placid yet observant pig on the other. Both figures gaze at the viewer, and the pig even appears to be intelligently listening. The spectator's angle of view is no longer that of a machine, but of a human. The pig and avatar seem reconciled to each other, perhaps even mutually affectionate; neither is concerned about being eaten. The thought arises—how different the painting would be if the *pig* in the title had been a dog. A friendship characterised by justice between man and pig is more impressive, because so much rarer.

I asked Andriu Deplazes if he had always wished to be a painter. No, he said. For a time, he had trained to be a classical musician, but turned away from music because there was something repellent about the need to demonstrate virtuosity. To be a virtuoso, as the moral world depicted in these paintings clearly shows, is not the same as having virtue. And yet, at the same time, there are still traces of virtuosity in Deplazes' practice: in the idealised landscapes that he renders, and in the easy depiction of animal life. It is only humans that he will not denigrate with such perfection. Their overpainted faces do not allow them to be captured as things, but rather present them as subjects. They elude categorisation because they are responding, in real time, to what they see in us.

List of Works

Cover
Five bodies in red-yellow light, 2021
Oil on canvas
160 × 190 cm

Inside Cover
Body on imaginary plants, 2021
Oil on canvas
44 × 52 cm

1 Body in bathtub, 2021
Oil on canvas
80 × 60 cm

2 Two bodies on stairs, 2021
Oil on canvas
190 × 140 cm

3 Body in bathroom, 2021
Oil on canvas
37 × 36 cm

4 Slackliner, 2021
Oil on canvas
207 × 315 cm

6 Body and flowers, 2021
Oil on canvas
93 × 77 cm

7 Two bunnies in front of four dandelions, 2021
Oil on canvas
37.5 × 28.5 cm

8 Body, stick and condensation trail, 2020
Oil on canvas
160 × 140 cm

9 Drone over water, 2021
Oil on canvas
45 × 62.5 cm

10 Six eyes in the horizon, 2021
Oil on canvas
168 × 224 cm

12 Body, sheep, and sofa, 2021
Oil on canvas
110 × 100 cm

13 Flower and mountains, 2019
Oil on canvas
41 × 33 cm

14 Body and pig sitting, 2021
Oil on canvas
59 × 43 cm

15 Body holding tree, 2019
Oil on canvas
130 × 150 cm

16 Stork in front of drone in scattered light, 2021
Oil on canvas
177 × 227 cm

18 Body and cow, 2021
Oil on canvas
196 × 243 cm

19 Hand on child's head, 2021
Oil on canvas
155 × 130 cm

20 Body with rifle, 2021
Oil on canvas
50 × 40 cm

21 Stand up paddle kneeling, 2020
Oil on canvas
100 × 125.5 cm

22 Stag and white vastness, 2020
Oil on canvas
120 × 185 cm

24 Eagle hunting drone, 2021
Oil on canvas
180 × 160 cm

25 Scalp on horizon, 2021
Oil on canvas
51 × 46 cm

26 Body holding rod, 2020
Oil on canvas
50 × 40 cm

27 Upper body and green trees, 2019
Oil and wax on canvas
46 × 51 cm

28 Two bodies, barge, leash and dog, 2020
Oil on canvas
207 × 327 cm

30 Light crossing, 2021
Oil on canvas
160 × 200 cm

31 Body in front of railing, 2020
Oil on canvas
45 × 41 cm

32 Bodies at table, 2021
Oil on canvas
194 × 248 cm

All Works are Courtesy the Artist
and Galerie Peter Kilchmann, Zurich
www.peterkilchmann.com

Andriu Deplazes
Bodies in Scattered Light

First Edition

Text by Adam Jasper
Lithography by Marjeta Morinc

Published by Nieves
www.nievesbooks.com

© 2021 Andriu Deplazes,
Galerie Peter Kilchmann and Nieves
Reproduction without permission prohibited

ISBN 978-3-907179-39-0

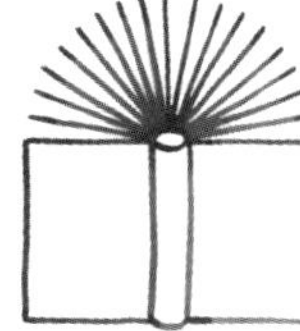

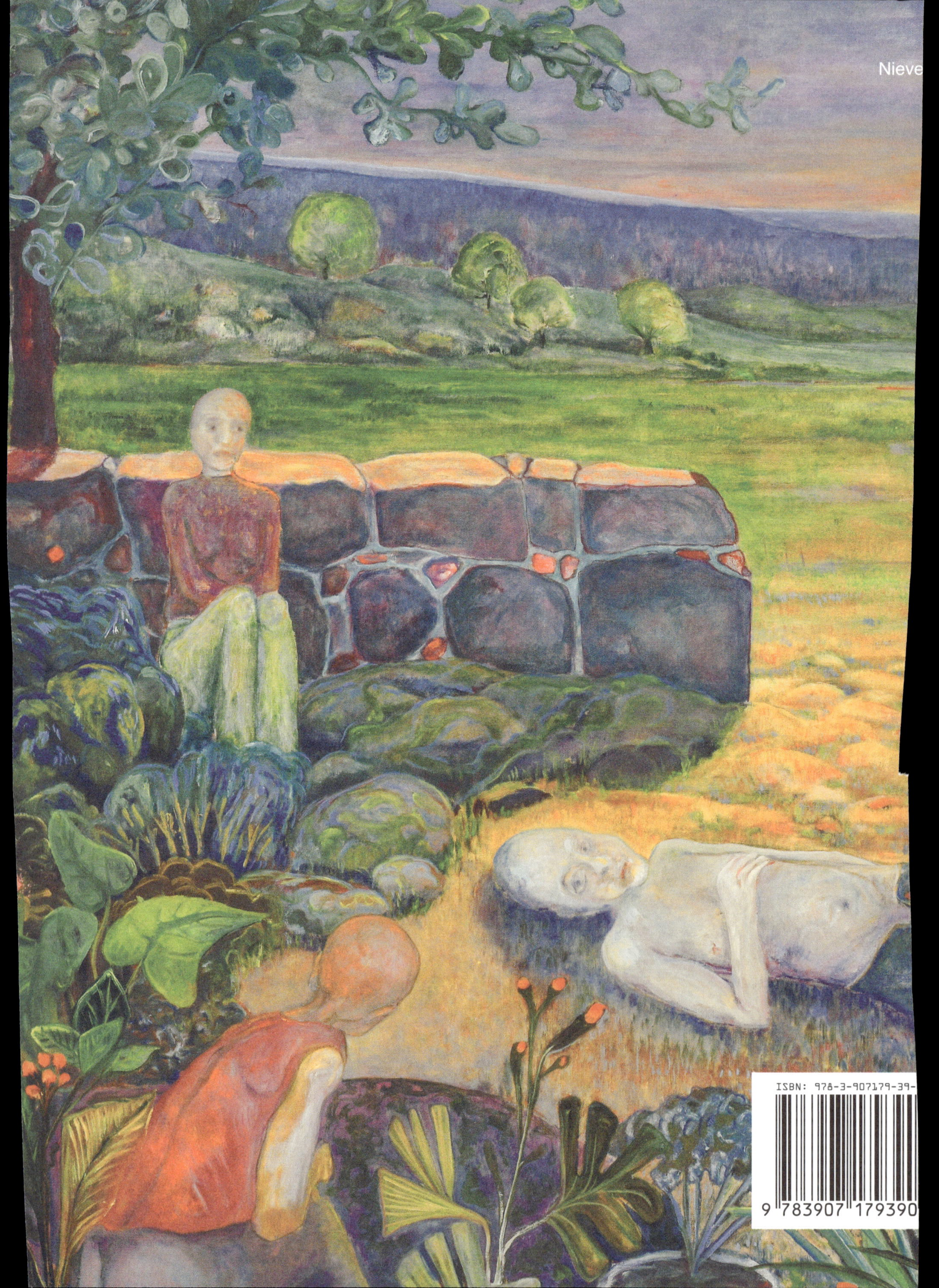
Nieve
ISBN: 978-3-907179-39-
9 783907 179390

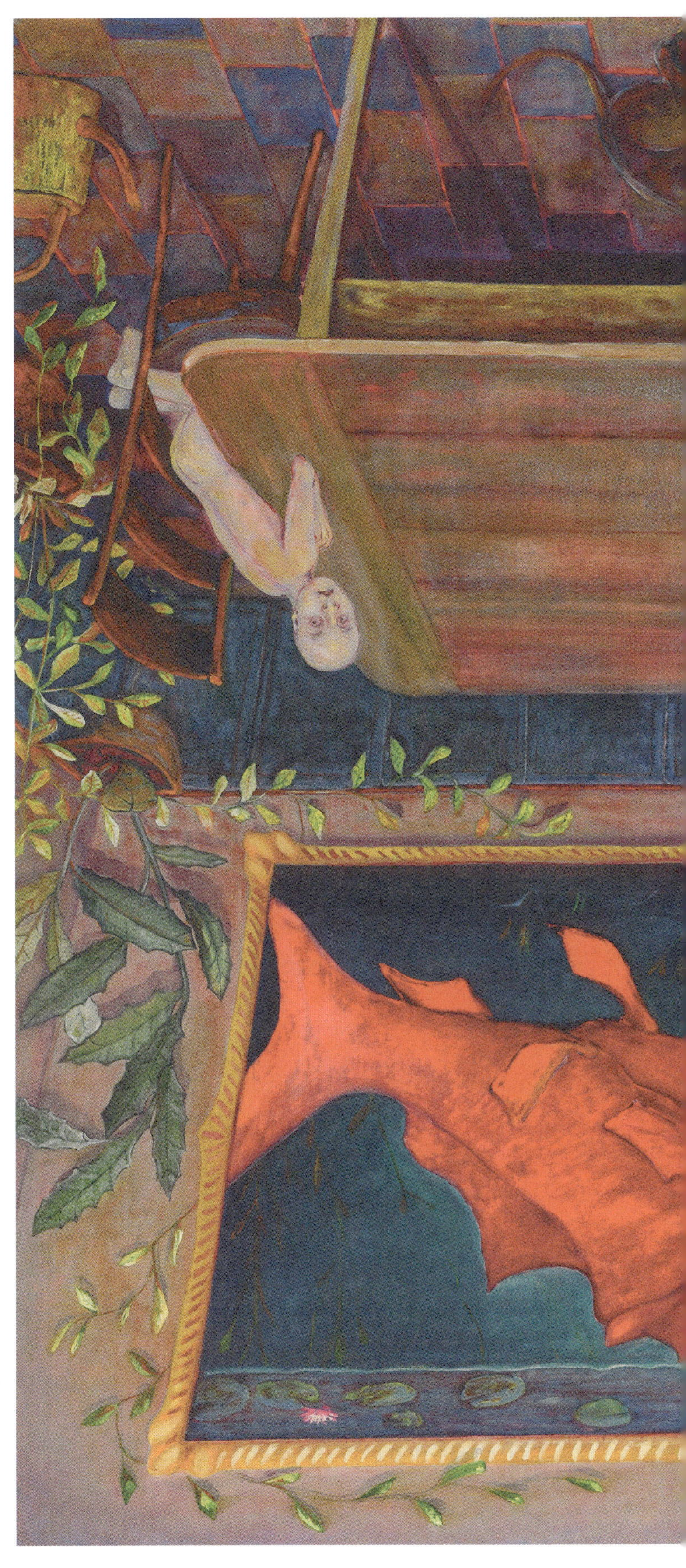

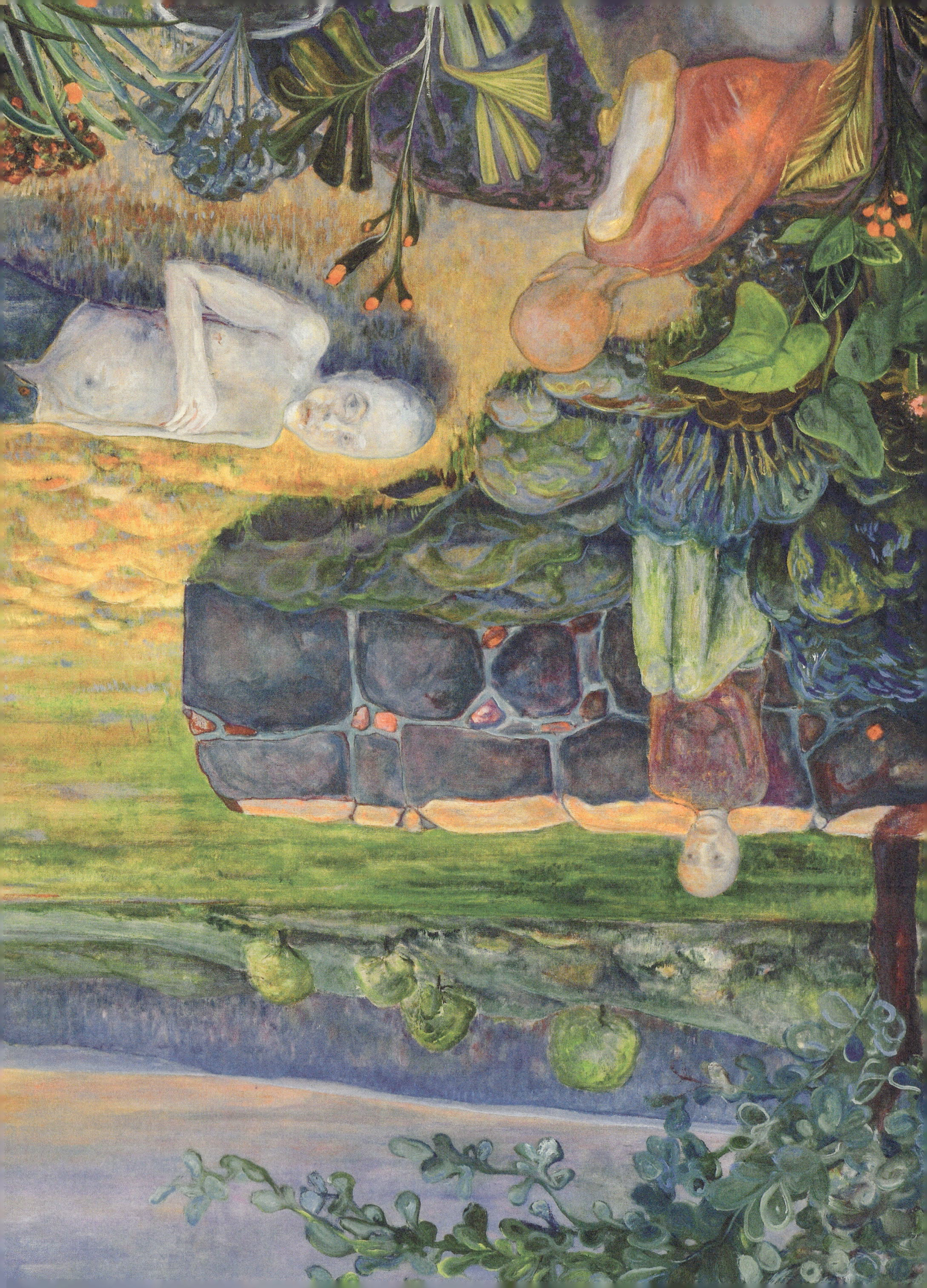